The Sacred Quest

Contributing Authors

Robert Atkinson

Jude Currivan

Charles Einstein

Ken D. Foster

Suzanne Giesemann

Adam C. Hall

Kurt Johnson

Commentary by Alexander Laszlo

Ervin Laszlo

David Lorimer

Ignazio Masulli

Bradley Nelson

Jon Ramer

Mária Sági

Mirela Sula

Alberto Villoldo

Shannon Winters

THE SACRED QUEST

BECOMING ONE ON PLANET EARTH

ERVIN LASZLO
WITH CONTRIBUTING AUTHORS
FOREWORD BY DARLENE GREEN
INTRODUCTION BY NEALE DONALD WALSCH

Waterside Productions

Copyright © 2025 by Ervin Laszlo

All rights reserved. This book or any portion thereof may not be reproduced or used in any manner whatsoever without the express written permission of the publisher except for the use of brief quotations in articles and book reviews.

NO AI TRAINING: Without in any way limiting the author's [and publisher's] exclusive rights under copyright, any use of this publication to "train" generative artificial intelligence (AI) technologies to generate text is expressly prohibited. The author reserves all rights to license uses of this work for generative AI training and development of machine learning language models.

First Printing, 2025

ISBN-13: 978-1-968401-12-2 print edition
ISBN-13: 978-1-968401-13-9 ebook edition

Waterside Productions
2055 Oxford Ave
Cardiff, CA 92007
www.waterside.com

*This is dedicated to my beautiful wife
Carita Laszlo
Our unwavering love and devotion have a powerful
influence on me, our family, my well-being, and
the success of my life's work.*

*This book is dedicated to all members of the human family
waking up to the amazing privilege and unique responsibility
of having been born a human being on planet earth.*

Note from the Author

As all thoughtful and responsible people, you must have asked yourselves, *Why am I here? Is there purpose and meaning to my existence?* This book gives a resounding yes. The purpose and the meaning underlying your existence are both personal and cosmic. What you think and what you do matter. They matter both to you and to the universe. It is your sacred duty to find out why they matter and to think and act in light of it.

The few minutes it will take you to read the gist of this book will inform your thinking and give meaning to your existence. Start with the conclusions of the classic statement in chapter one, and continue with the conclusions of the chapters that follow. Write up your queries in a few words and share them with us. This writer or his team promise to respond to reasonable demands to the best of their time and ability.

—Ervin Laszlo

Acknowledgments

I would like to first and foremost thank Nóra Csiszár, executive coordinator, who has been in constant service to me, my numerous projects, and making sure all pieces of the puzzle are in place at all times. This is a tireless job she does without hesitation. I am grateful beyond words for her tenacity and brilliant abilities to constantly create success.

To the many on this sacred quest journey, it would take my lifetime to mention. I thank you for your heartfelt commitment to the future of humanity. There are the members of the Club of Budapest, those dedicated on my many summits at the Laszlo Institute of New Paradigm Research, and all those reading this book. You know who you are, and you are doing what is required to becoming one on planet earth. Thank you.

Many thanks to Gayle Gladstone at Waterside Productions for making sure publications go out and are represented throughout the world. We are great friends.

I would also like to thank Kurt Johnson, Ariel Patricia, and Light on Light Press for believing in this sacred quest.

Letter from the Publisher

We honor Ervin Laszlo with gratitude and admiration, whose life's work laid the foundation for *The Sacred Quest*.

A pioneer of systems science and a leading voice in the evolution of consciousness, Dr. Laszlo has spent a lifetime illuminating our deep connection to one another and to the living universe. This volume emerges from his enduring call to reawaken our sacred responsibility—to each other, to the earth, and to the deeper intelligence that connects all things.

His clarity, courage, and wisdom have guided not only the spirit of this book but the movement it represents. We are privileged to include his voice here—and to walk a path he has long helped to light.

Gayle Gladstone

The Message of This Book

The ancient naturalists had a saying based evidently on profound observation. *Natura Naturans*, nature not merely "is" but "becomes." Nature is "naturing." We need to add humanity to this insight. Humanity, too, needs to be naturing, becoming coherent and one with the living world.

Humanitas Naturans: this motto designates an aim worthy of our most earnest attention.

Driven by the hunger for power and wealth and enabled by new technology, the human community is evermore separating itself from the world in which it has come to be. We are losing the race with the processes that we have inadvertently launched; the world around us and our own being in the world are becoming more and more unsustainable. If we continue on this path, we risk growing crises and a major breakdown.

We need to change. This does not merely call for creating and obeying a few ecological commands, important as they are: it calls for new aspirations and a new pattern of behavior in the human community as a whole. The Call is for an essentially changed human presence on the planet. To use the metaphor featured in this book, we need to learn to dance not just *on* the planet, but *with* the planet.

The human being we need is already emerging among the people of the young generations. We need to embrace, intensify, and accelerate its emergence. The book in front of the reader is dedicated to achieving this truly sacred quest. It offers the sense of being an integral and conscious part of the evolution that unfolds in nature and the universe, and it would also unfold on this planet if our shortsighted aspirations do not block it.

As conscious members of the human community, we need to wake up to our powers as well as our responsibilities. The reader will encounter all that he or she needs to advance this cause in the context of a co-evolving, participatory world. Undertaking this challenge is the sacred quest to which this book is dedicated.

The vision of a better world beckons, and we can and surely will realize it. But if we are to do so in our lifetime, we need more wisdom and greater perseverance. These essential attributes are cited on the pages that follow. These pages are contributed by a small group of eminent thought leaders, and are addressed, as the call proclaimed here states, to all who are open to comprehending and adopting our sacred quest.

The imperative of our day is to awaken to the awesome privilege as well as unique responsibility of having been born a human being on planet earth.

Table of Contents

Foreword
Darlene Green xxi

Introduction
Neale Donald Walsch xxv

The Essential Insights xxix

The Essential Actions.. xxxiii

Part 1:
VISIONING A CONSCIOUS EVOLUTION

Chapter One
The Sacred Quest
Ervin Laszlo... 3

Chapter Two
Evolution: The New Story from Science
Charles Eisenstein.. 18

Chapter Three
The Cosmic Meaning and Purpose of Humanity's Sacred Quest
Jude Currivan. 26

Chapter Four
Our Sacred Quest and the Quest for a Universal Spirituality
Robert Atkinson... 41

Chapter Five
Humanity's Sacred Quest in the Historical Perspective
Ignazio Masulli.. 52

Chapter Six
Dream the Sacred Dream: the American Wisdom Traditions and the Sacred Quest of Contemporary Humanity
Alberto Villoldo 63

Chapter Seven
Our Quest in the Vision of Spiritual Master Peter Deunov
David Lorimer 67

Part 2:
THE SACRED ACTIONS

Chapter Eight
Activate Your Sacred Quest
Adam C. Hall.. 79

Chapter Nine
Enlisting Feminine Power in Pursuing Our Sacred Quest
Mirela Sula... 100

Chapter Ten
Healing As a Sacred Quest
Mária Sági.. 108

Chapter Eleven
Taking Down the Walls Around Our Heart
Bradley Nelson. 118

Chapter Twelve
Bringing Our Sacred Quest Home
Suzanne Giesemann. 125

CONCLUDING REFLECTIONS AND EXPLORATIONS

More on the New Story Inspiring and Supporting
Our Sacred Quest
Robert Atkinson, Shannon Winters, and Kurt Johnson. 145

To Dance Our Sacred Dance: Practical Advice
from a Personal Transformation Coach
Ken D. Foster 151

Uniting Humanity: Wisdom and Technology for a New Era
Jon Ramer 169

The Principal and Contributing Authors' Bios 177

Throughout history, many of the greatest scientific minds, from Kepler and Newton to Einstein and Planck, found that the deeper they explored the nature of reality, the more they encountered a profound order and mystery underlying the universe. Their discoveries often opened new dialogue between science and the sacred.

In *The Sacred Quest*, Ervin Laszlo, together with a circle of visionary thinkers, extends this inquiry by exploring how a deeper understanding of the cosmos may guide humanity toward a renewed awareness of our interconnectedness and our shared responsibility for life on earth.

FOREWORD

The Sacred Quest: A Clarion Call

Humanity stands at a profound evolutionary threshold. The tidal shift of transformation is underway. Mirroring a rapidly transitioning landscape, we are invited to a greater state of awareness.

Ervin Laszlo's *The Sacred Quest: Becoming One on Planet Earth* offers clarity. The questions asked by humanity reflect an existential search. Who am I? Who are we within this vast universe? What is the nature of the intelligence that animates life? And how might we coexist in a state of harmony? *The Sacred Quest* speaks to the deep yearning within humanity to discover meaning, purpose, and connection. It calls us to expand our awareness beyond the boundaries of separation and to recognize the profound unity that binds all existence.

Throughout his extensive and distinguished career, Ervin Laszlo has illuminated the patterns that connect science, systems theory, and consciousness. In this book he invites readers to recognize that evolution is an ongoing process in which humanity plays a role. We are not passive observers but conscious participants capable of transcending limitations of the past and helping guide the direction of our collective future in rhythm with the universe.

The evolutionary horizon continually reveals new ground. The past does not define the future into which we are now growing. The movement of life is always toward greater wholeness, inviting each of us into the next expression of our being. With this elevation of consciousness comes a greater sense of peace and coherence, as heart and soul align in new ways to create and participate in the unfolding of life.

Humanity has outgrown perceptions and assumptions that once shaped our understanding of reality. What awaits is a deeper experience accessing the divine wisdom that resides within us, beyond perceived limitations of the past. *The Sacred Quest* is a call not only to awaken to the responsibility we hold as the collective of humanity, but to move forward consciously and courageously through action.

> *"The emerging universal truth is that love is the expression of cosmic holotropism of all things that evolve in space and time. The evolution of the things that emerge in the universe is none other than the manifestation of the attraction toward oneness of the beings that came to grace our planet."*
> —Ervin Laszlo, *The Sacred Quest*

What becomes available as we live from the synergy of wholeness into the consciousness of Oneness, naturally sourced by Love? We already possess everything required for the next step of realization. However, this is not a passive process. We must reach for our better selves and consciously participate in the emergence of who we are becoming.

The vista of wholeness offers a vast perspective and context. From here we recognize the undeniable interconnectedness of all life. The state of Oneness holds the clear and present call to take responsibility for each other and our beautiful earth. As we stand in the light of our most authentic expression, we have access to the wisdom, clarity, love, and compassion needed to create our new world together.

With the turning of each page, you will be invited to explore a vision of humanity's future rooted in unity, responsibility, and awakened consciousness. In *The Sacred Quest*, Ervin Laszlo opens a doorway into a deeper understanding of who we are and what we may yet become. This is ultimately the journey of revealing the inextricable connection of all life and the wisdom accessed through our own consciousness. The future of our world depends on the awareness we bring to this moment.

The perspectives of science and sacred point toward the same horizon: a humanity awakening to its deeper nature and discovering that evolution is not an abstract theory, but a living process expressing within each of us.

Love invites a new listening, reminding humanity of the power of our own voice and to participate consciously in the sacred unfolding of our path forward together.

The invitation is before us.
And the journey has begun.
In Appreciation,
Darlene Green
Author of: The *In Service to Love* trilogy
and *Love Speaks, Always*

INTRODUCTION

NEALE DONALD WALSCH

Was Bill right? Did this wonderful friend of humanity and the arts have his finger on something really important when he wrote into the dialogue of his most famous play: "There are more things in Heaven and Earth, Horatio, than are dreamt of in your philosophy."

William Shakespeare put it more dramatically, perhaps, but in no way more directly, emphatically, or importantly than another of humanity's friends—perhaps one of its best friends ever—Ervin Laszlo, who has created a fabulous and fascinating focus with his own words on these pages, over five hundred years later: "There is a reason for the existence of conscious species on earth. We are not here by chance."

Human beings have been asking by the billions for thousands of years what that reason *is*. "Why am I here?" We have begged to know, "What am I doing in this place?"

Most of us have been inundated with the ideas held by many within our species in answer to those questions. None of those notions, however, came close to revealing what I discovered only later in life to be the truth.

There was a formula that I saw people among my family and friends living in from age eighteen to eighty, and that I slipped into adopting myself without even consciously choosing it. Then, about midway through that timeline, I came to a staggering realization. I saw that my life had little to do with very much that really mattered. I mean, outside of my own little "tent"; that private enclosure of activity in which I lived.

I wasn't really happy there much of the time. I wasn't feeling fulfilled in the larger ways that I somehow felt, and intuitively knew, that Life could provide.

What was it that I was somehow sensing? If I was asked now, I would put it into nine words: "There's more going on here than meets the eye."

Well, as it happens, I *was* asked now, by Ervin Laszlo himself, who kindly invited me to write an introduction to this remarkable book. I am grateful to him for the opportunity because it gives me a chance to emphasize—in another forum and in another way—the life-changing realization I came to after thirty years of adult life. I'm referring to the message I experienced myself as having received from the Source of Divine Wisdom that speaks to all of us from a place deep within. I have felt urged, ever since, to share this message with as many people as possible, because of what I consider to be its significance:

We are all One.

There is only One Thing, and we are all part of The One Thing There Is.

If I were to rank, in terms of their potential positive impact on our world and the well-being of its people, what I was told in what I have understood to be my own conversations with God, I would surely put this one near the top.

The only message from that dialogue I would put above it is the Divine revelation that no human being on this planet is simply a Body with a Mind, but that all people are spiritual entities—called Souls—traveling through life *with* a Body and a Mind for a *reason.*

(Yes, exactly what Ervin has said.)

That reason, it has been made clear to me, is to serve what I have been told is The Agenda of the Soul. And that Agenda is the same for every person across the globe. Put into one word: *EVOLUTION.*

This is a word describing the advancing development of not just each individual, but of our entire species—and note this ... *of the planet itself.* All of Life is evolving to become a greater representation (that is, a grander *re-presentation*) of its Originating Source, which some of us call "God."

The beauty of what Ervin Laszlo has done here is to take this idea out of the realm of the purely spiritual and bring it home to all of us in the language of *basic science.* He has made something dismissed by many as merely esoteric, and turned it into that which is meaningfully realistic, and can therefore be embraced by people of every persuasion, whether they consider themselves religiously inclined, faith-based, or not.

Ah! At last! Something that ALL OF US can relate to. A reason that makes sense to the Body, the Mind, *and* the Soul, not just one of the three.

Ervin tells us here that living systems evolve in accordance with a specific "wholeness-oriented" and "wholeness-creating" tendency in nature. In other words, that which *Conversations with God* calls "oneness" is part of Life's *system* and Life's *process.* And our continual, intentional, motivated involvement in that unfolding through the creation, expression, embracing, and demonstration of Oneness is the sacred quest of our existence on earth.

It is, in fact, our *raison d'être.*

At a deep level, and committing to it in a purposeful way, can change one's life for the better, and can transform in wondrous ways how our entire species evolves. I can think of no better reason to delve into this book.

THE ESSENTIAL INSIGHTS

BY ERVIN LASZLO
IN SHADED BOXES FOLLOWED BY COMMENTARY BY
ALEXANDER LASZLO

THE CRUCIAL INSIGHT

> To be a human on earth is an awesome privilege as well as an ineluctable responsibility. Recognizing this insight is crucial for human persistence in the embrace of the evolution of life on planet earth.

What It Means: Understanding Humanity's Sacred Quest
Are humans somehow more special, privileged, and important than other beings on earth? Absolutely not. And yet ... there are things humans can do that no other creature on earth can. We can empathize with *all creatures* on the planet. We know what it's like to fly, to live under the water, in the desert, underground, microscopically, and as entire hives, forests, and mountains. We can relate ... and beyond that, we can *connect.* We can connect life with life and—when we do it with joy and love, like facilitating a great conversation among old friends—we *augment* all life.

How to Do It: Activating Our Understanding of Humanity's Sacred Quest

If you like a good story, then you already know how to do this. But it helps if you know what to listen for, and how to say things, once you're dialed in. The best way to learn is to listen; nature and the cosmos that nurtures nature have a way of talking that we often miss—usually because we're too busy staring at our phones, at our own reflections, or simply just spacing out. But there's a kind of "Gaia Talk" that is all the time forming and informing us. And it's a reciprocal thing! So, as we practice Gaia Talk (which is 99 percent listening and 1 percent actually talking), we participate as connectors and augmenters of life.

> Living up to the responsibility entailed by being human is a sacred quest for all members of the human family. It is to avert the specter of growing crises and ultimate extinction, opening instead the path to harmonious existence and continued evolution for humanity. The ultimate objective of this quest is to regain humanity's coherence with planet and universe.

What It Means

Rhythm, balance, flow. These are integral to Gaia Talk. By and large, humanity has fallen out of rhythm, lost balance, and ceased to flow with the greater narratives that sustain all life on earth. Regaining our balance is not only in our own best interest, but also what we are called to do as connectors and augmenters of life—what only we can do on earth. As we regain our footing and learn to dance the dance of life—*with* life and *as* life—we come into our own as a planetary species. We self-actualize and realize our full potential at the next stage of our collective evolution as a species. This is our destiny—if we are not deaf to the call to fulfill it.

How to Do It
Cultivating our sense-abilities, and through them, our response-abilities as co-creators of future-creating, life-affirming, and opportunity-increasing ways of being—that's what it takes to live up to the responsibility of becoming evolutionary co-creators. Choosing paths of being and becoming that connect and augment life is as natural, simple, and effortless as breathing. But we've forgotten how to breathe and be breathed into life on earth! Listening and trusting the natural flow of life, not just of human life, but of *life writ large* ... that's the ticket to a harmonious and fully engaged human presence on earth.

> The choice between extinction and evolution rests with contemporary humans, in particular with the mindset adopted by a critical mass of conscious individuals. The transformation of the current mindset to include insights such as our ineluctable responsibility for life and well-being on the planet is a task awaiting all of us.

What It Means
Anyone who looks at the role humans are playing on earth in terms of the impact we are having will most likely conclude that we are some sort of planetary parasite, slowly killing our host as we suck life from it. But even if

that's the way things look at the broad-brush scale, there is also so much good that we are doing already now! We just have to get better at doing it … upshifting our consciousness (our mindset, our heartset, and our handset) for what a world that works for all can be like. A dream? An ideal? An illusion? Not in the least! It is the evolutionary imperative of our time.

How to Do It

The good news is that we don't have to try to engage in an upshift of consciousness all by ourselves. In fact, it wouldn't make any difference even if we were able to. This is a time for *collective intelligence* (and we really have all the tools and technologies to make it happen). But for collective intelligence to work, we must first engage in *connective intelligence.* This means learning to connect life with life—in all ways. But even that is not enough by itself. For connective intelligence to augment life, we must cultivate *empathetic intelligence* too. It is easy and fun to practice these forms of relationality, of greater relational intelligence. After all, it's just like breathing (and being breathed) into life. We really do know how.

THE ESSENTIAL ACTIONS:

Accessing and Activating Our Innate Evolutionary Impetus

> The universe's innate evolutionary impetus is humanity's guide toward a coherent love- and consciousness-imbued existence on planet earth. To access and activate this subtle but real impetus, we must address the deep layers of our consciousness.

What It Means
Once we recognize that we are not smarter than nature (and that we don't have to keep trying to prove we are), we can relearn how to flow, regain our balance with nature, and realign with the rhythms that create thriving, flourishing, and celebratory patterns of life. This is the underlying pattern of nature, and indeed, of cosmic evolution. We don't stand outside of this dynamic, nor can we warp it to our own designs without adverse long-term effect. What a relief once we realize that we can flow *with* nature, rather than constantly worrying about how to make it flow!

How to Do It
Knowing that we are true expressions of an integral and interdependent narrative of life on earth starts us down a path of learning to harmonize, to connect, to augment, and to celebrate all life. Taking on the mantle of evolutionary co-creators of life on earth is not a job of

overlords. Quite the opposite! It is a job of curators, of lovers of life and beauty and all things that augment life. It is a matter of joining *with* life, not seeking to dominate or subjugate it. When we put a little effort into taking care of nature, we find the favor returned ten-fold!

> We need to overcome all elements of noise that would interfere with receiving this vital signal: the urgent need to perceive and activate the evolutionary impetus present in our life and consciousness.

What It Means
As a species, we are often hypnotized by our own power and ability to make, do, shape, and redirect life and the living world around us. But in our mad dash to a mechanized nirvana, we have lost touch with the essential balance of the world. The more we try to bring it into balance, the more we find ourselves with short-term gains and bigger and bigger problems of imbalance. Learning to slow down, to listen, to care for the subtle, life-giving dynamics of nature is at the heart of the upshift in consciousness that our species is engaging in right now.

How to Do It
Grasping for answers, searching for solutions to problems of our own making, trying to fix nature so that it is more to our liking … these are all ways of being that do not connect life with life and, in the end, disconnect and diminish our hope of greater harmony in, with, and through nature. Just making yourself available to the life-affirming, future-creating, and opportunity-increasing patterns that constantly flow us into existence can help us take on

the mantle of evolutionary co-creators. Breathing deep, opening ourselves to Gaia Talk, allowing ourselves to be danced by the patterns that bring forth the abundance that fills the earth with life ... this is how we teem with evolutionary potential.

> The perception of this impetus can be cultivated. Upon experiencing some form of joy and satisfaction in finding syntony, harmony, and sympathy among divers elements our consciousness is naturally filled with a sense of wholeness. Consciously applying this sensation is to project an attraction toward wholeness and love in our life and surrounding. By activating our innate impetus, we are advancing the evolution of life in this region of the universe. The experience of joy and satisfaction can be enhanced by consciously grasping it and applying it to similar conditions throughout the range of our experience. Thus, our own consciousness harbors the key to creating higher levels of wholeness and coherence in our world.

What It Means
Our evolutionary history has prepared us perfectly to live into this moment of our higher potential. We have full evolutionary competency to curate life on earth as connectors and augmenters of a thriving world! There is nothing to fix, no technology to invent, indeed, nothing missing at all. Except, that is, our willingness to align with the deeper evolutionary flows of being and becoming that constantly bring us into relationship with life. Learning how to navigate those flows and how to dance with—and be danced by—them, that is the task before us now.

How to Do It
Fostering relational intelligence (the empathetic intelligence that potentiates our connective intelligence and sets our collective intelligence in service of thrivable futures) starts with listening, connecting, and augmenting our relationship first and foremost with ourselves. Yes, we must first learn to be in thriving balance with our own bodies, our emotions, our thoughts, and our own well-being. Then we can turn to being in right relationship with others, fostering functional relationships with friends, family, coworkers, and neighbors. Beyond that, we can practice being in flow with the more-than-human world that surrounds and sustains us. As we learn the ways of syntony inherent in Gaia Talk, we come into thriving relationship with our ancestors and all those who have come before us, honoring what they have done to bring us to this moment of life. At the same time, we can learn to be good "future ancestors" ourselves, recognizing that we are "ancestors in training" right now, scaffolding the potential of future generations to thrive. And finally, we can use your syntony sense to expand our fluency in Gaia Talk beyond the confines of our planet, recognizing the greater cosmic narrative that undergirds and potentiates patterns of wholeness and coherence throughout the universe. These five spheres of practice—from the *intra-personal* to the *inter-personal* to the *trans-species* to the *trans-generational* to the *pan-cosmic*—these comprise the practice ground to upshift our being and inter-being as evolutionary co-creators.

> Liberating our minds to open the path to perceiving our innate evolutionary impetus is the first step. It

needs to be followed by the courage and determination to act on our perception of this impetus. There could not be a clearer and more urgent quest for responsible individuals than purposively spreading the joy, satisfaction, and love accompanying the perception of the evolutionary impetus. This will inform and inspire the mindset that dominates the thinking and the actions of contemporary humanity.

What It Means

While the need is both urgent and important, we don't have to carry the burden of changing the world all on our own shoulders. Not individually. Not even as an urgent need to somehow become the majority of humanity. Even a small group of dedicated individuals—in harmony with nature and their living environment—can turn the tide. Indeed, this is the way nature works. It's not a matter of convincing others, of selling the idea, of mounting a campaign. We can do this quietly, in our own ways, in our own worlds—but not in isolation. Never in isolation! Connecting life with life and augmenting the potential of life to thrive—this can be done in myriad ways. The important thing is to do it. Not just to talk about it or to try to convince others to connect and augment life and the life-giving processes all around them. Just doing it is all it takes.

How to Do It

How do friendships start? How does a forest grow? What makes a garden bloom? These are all matters of relational intelligence, and they cannot be learned except through immersion in the patterns of syntony that form and inform life on earth in the native language of Gaia Talk. The good thing is that nature is constantly speaking this language all around us, so we are swimming in these patterns all the time. But to recognize them and work with them, we must first *stop*—get out of our own way. Then we can more easily *connect*—sense into what is seeking to emerge. And that makes us more able to *flow*—to align with the pulse of change that is life-affirming, future-creating, and opportunity-increasing. For all life. Now and into the future. This is our sacred quest. The time for it is now. And you … you are here now. It is your time.

The Ultimate Insight
Some thirteen billion years ago, a cosmic singularity collapsed the seamless wholeness that presumably characterized the primeval universe. The holotropism we find in nature and consciousness is an indication that the universe is actively seeking to recover its pre-collapse wholeness. The objective of achieving coherence in us and around us is a sacred quest of truly cosmic significance.

The Humanity's Sacred Quest Program of the Laszlo Institute of New Paradigm Research is dedicated to achieving the crucially important quest of receiving and activating the evolutionary impetus innate in us as in all beings on the planet. We aim to achieve this end in close collaboration with advanced thinking groups and organizations the world over.

Accepting this quest is the basic precondition for creating a movement that lifts humanity beyond its current stage of crises and collapse to the next level of its planetary evolution.

Part 1

VISIONING A CONSCIOUS EVOLUTION

CHAPTER ONE
THE SACRED QUEST

ERVIN LASZLO

We are, as far as we know, the most evolved form of life in this corner of the universe. We can, if we so wish, guide our own evolution. We can, if we so decide, evolve in harmony with the planet. But will we do so? We may be the most highly evolved, but not necessarily the best evolved form of life on earth. Will we have the wisdom to upshift our further evolution to the planet?

We do not as yet have an answer to this crucial question. But we do know that the answer *could* be positive. Making it positive is a responsibility. This is a planetary, indeed a cosmic responsibility—it may decide the fate of the higher forms of life, and of the consciousness associated with them, on the planet. Creating the conditions that enable us to give a positive answer is more than an everyday responsibility. It is a quest. A sacred quest.

We need to wake up and meet our sacred quest. This is not a quixotic endeavor. We have the information, the skills, and the technologies. We need to come up with the will, the courage, to evolve in harmony with the planet.

Is it *our* responsibility to recognize and act on this sacred quest? Evidently, this should be the responsibility of the human community as such. But to wait for the human community to act in time would be naïve and irresponsible. Awakened individuals in that community need to take matters into their own hands. The sacred quest of humanity is *our* quest. Yours and mine.

Is it reasonable to expect us to wake up and meet this quest? There are preconditions for accepting to perform a task, sacred or not. It concerns the reasonability of the demand to act. As philosophers point out, "*ought* implies *can*." It is not reasonable to demand something of us if performing that task is beyond our ability. The human community itself cannot be responsible for meeting this sacred quest because at this point of its evolutionary history, the human community cannot act purposively to satisfy this, or indeed any, demand. Only individual members of that community can act in regard to such a demand. A further advance would need to be reached in our evolution to render the human community itself capable of purposive action.

The reasonable demand to act is not to be addressed to the human community, it is to be addressed to awakened members of that community.

Clearly, individuals cannot be asked to meet humanity's sacred quest by themselves. But they could bring together cohesive groups, and these groups could act effectively. A quote that is attributed to famed anthropologist Margaret Mead is, "Never doubt that a small group of thoughtful, committed citizens can change the world. Indeed, it's the only thing that ever has." We could require of a critical mass of awakened individuals to accept humanity's sacred quest.

Ever more people are coming to the insight that acting in tune with the planet is what they need to do, and this may offer the best way to live and evolve on this planet. Consciously guided evolution could be the way forward.

The New Story of Evolution

After decades and even centuries of increasingly adamant but fruitless debate, it has become accepted that life on earth was not *created*. It has *evolved*. The question is not *whether* life has evolved, only *how* it has evolved.

For classical Darwinism, the evolution of life is a fortunate happenstance—a chance combination of genes exposed to natural selection. We are here by chance, and we will either remain here by chance or disappear by chance. Nothing on this score can be done to guide this process by human action.

However, there is a new story of evolution emerging in the natural sciences. This is a different story. We are on earth not by chance, but as a consequence of the evolution that unfolds here and presumably throughout the universe. Our existence testifies to a fundamental process. Life is not a product of random interactions.

The new story shifts the evolution of living species from mere chance to the unfolding of a purposive process. The presence of life is testimony that there is more than chance involved in the evolution of life. Life is a natural consequence of the unfolding of a fundamental, and as it appears universal, process in nature. It is a purposive, even if it is not a consciousness-guided, process. This process favors the creation of complex entities of integral coherence.

The new story is a radical innovation in the life sciences. Until now, the mainstream life science community did not admit a discoverable tendency that would orient the evolution of life. Scientists suspected that recognizing a guiding principle behind evolution would lead to a return to vitalism: the assumption that a higher intelligence or force directs the evolution of life. This suspicion proved unfounded. We now know that we can have systems that are goal-directed without being consciously guided. Information technology describes such systems, and they occur in nature as well. Goal-directedness does not call for an external guiding principle. The process is guided by the systems themselves.

The new story is that evolution on earth does not rely on external guidance. Evolution is guided by an innate impetus in nature.

A Closer Look at the New Story of Evolution

The recognition that evolution is guided by an innate impetus is a radical innovation in the natural sciences. It changes the concept of life. Living systems are intrinsically goal-originated and goal-directed. They are neither externally directed nor are they the product of chance interactions.

The old story of evolution was limited to the genetic evolution of biological species. According to the old story, there is no higher purpose behind the evolution of life on earth. Vitalism, the philosophy that there is, is a faulty concept.

But if we reject vitalism as the explanation of the evolution we experience, what are we left with? We are left with the tenet that our existence, the existence of life altogether, is a chance occurrence. A random shuffling of genes and molecules produced life as an unintended by-product. Life is a kind of fancy rust on the surface of the planet. It comes about through the random variation of macromolecular and genetic substances subjected to natural selection. In the course of time, the random iteration of genetic substances hits on configurations that are more resistant to change than most of the others. These "fit" configurations are selected by a natural process that eliminates the less fit alternatives. Some among these configurations prove capable of reproduction. They replace components that are no longer contributing to the persistence of the configuration itself. They manifest the phenomenon we identify as "life."

For the old story, the evolution of life is a process of random variation among genetic substances exposed to natural selection. This process does not admit to exceptions. The fittest survive and the rest pass into oblivion.

The old story, however, is not the last word. Another story offers a more plausible alternative. Evolution is intrinsically oriented toward creating particular kinds of systems. *There is an innate attraction built into the universe.* Evolution in space and time is *purposive*, but not consciously *purposeful*. We and other living systems are goal-originated and goal-oriented systems. We owe our existence neither to chance nor to higher guidance.

The argument against chance is backed by compelling evidence. A random shuffling of atoms and molecules could not have achieved the order and coherence we now find in.

Yet this alone is not a reason to invoke the power of a transcendental will. Life evolves as a result of the non-random emergence of configurations of genetic components on suitable planetary surfaces. The goal-orientation responsible for the presence of coherent configurations is innate to the universe itself.

The old story of evolution has been transcended. Living systems evolve on the basis of constraints and possibilities in nature, and are neither the result of transcendental intervention nor a random shuffling of genes. Life originates in the creative interplay of constraints and potentials unfolding in the universe.

Holotropism in the Universe

The new story of evolution identifies the kind of constraints and potentials that shape evolution on earth. An insight is born—complex systems evolve in accordance with a wholeness-oriented and wholeness-creating impetus innate to the universe. There is a statistically significant tendency toward the formation of complex configurations of molecular and genetic materials. The emerging configurations are not mere heaps or aggregates of the materials on which they are based. They are complex and coherent systems, resulting from the evolutionary impetus present in the universe.

The impetus toward complexity and coherence is a fundamental feature of the domains of life. The molecular and genetic materials that form higher-level systems are complex yet exhibit integral coherence. Here "integral" indicates that the systems bring together individually diverse elements, and "coherence" means that the elements in the system are fine-tuned to affect and respond to each other. Together they affect and respond to their environment.

The evolution of living systems testifies to an intrinsic impetus toward integrality among individually distinct and varied but interconnected molecular, genetic and cellular materials. There is a fundamental trend in space and time toward complexity and coherence. It leads to the formation of integrally coherent self-maintaining "living" systems. This process is not externally guided. It is an innate attraction in the universe.

The evolution of living systems proves to be a universal process. Life evolves in myriad places on this planet and throughout the universe, even under relatively unfavorable conditions. Organic macromolecules, the basic building blocks of living organisms, have been found even in interstellar space and even in the vicinity of active stars. They are found in the depths of profound seas and on the edges of active volcanoes. Not just organic molecules, entire organisms, so-called extremophiles, emerge under a wide variety of conditions.

The impetus to form coherent and complex systems is a manifestation of an innate attraction for integral coherence in nature. This accounts for the puzzle of how living systems could have emerged in the time that was available for evolution in the universe. A growing number of physical cosmologies suggest that the universe is both spatially and temporally finite though unbounded. In light of the known timeframe, this creates a puzzle. The time for evolutionary processes to produce the forms and levels of complex coherence we observe was about 13.8 billion years: the time that elapsed since the Big Bang.

This in itself enormous span of time is insufficient to have brought about the kind of systems that now populate the planet by random interactions. In this period, chance interactions, such as the unconstrained mixing of genetic materials, are not likely to have produced anything more complex than moss and blue-green algae. Cosmological physicist Sir Fred Hoyle remarked that the probability of living organisms emerging through a random mixing of their genes is similar to the probability that a hurricane blowing through a scrapyard assembles a working airplane.

The alternative to the old story is neither serendipity nor intervention by a transcendent intelligence. It is the recognition that an innate impetus is present in space and time. It biases otherwise random interactions and introduces a vector—an arrow of time—in the unfolding of evolutionary processes in the universe.

This furnishes the simplest and most compelling explanation of the evolution we observe. We can now identify the innate impetus: it is an integral wholeness-creating "attractor" in space and time: the *holotropic attractor*. (Attractors are conceptual entities that account for nonrandom behavior in complex systems, capable of accounting even for chaos as a complex form of order.) The physically effective but in-itself nonphysical attractor creates a subtle bias in interactions among atomic, molecular, and cellular materials. It increases the probability that complex, integrally coherent systems emerge wherever conditions permit. They emerge, as we have seen, even under relatively unfavorable conditions.

Physical cosmologies offer evidence that holotropism was present already in the early phases of the evolutionary process. Evolution in the universe began with the formation of hydrogen nuclei and continued with the synthesis of the atoms of the elements. The nonrandom formation of coherent systems began immediately in the wake of the Big Bang. Atoms form higher-order systems through the exclusion of electrons from all but the permissible energy shells around their nucleus. This so-called Pauli Exclusion Principle accounts for the integration of free electrons in specific energy shells or "clouds" and for their exclusion from alternative shells. The structure that results is not a heap of randomly assembled elements, but a coherent system: the kind of system that populates the periodic table of the elements. The systems that emerge combine selectively to form more complex and coherent ensembles: molecules and macromolecules. Macromolecules combine in turn and form cells and ensembles of cells. In the course of time these combine in turn and form still higher-order multicellular systems: groups and clusters of biological organisms.

Holotropism is a fundamental property of the universe. Its consequence is a process that shifts the dominant character of physical reality from randomness and disorder to forms and levels of order. In terms of classical Greek cosmology, the observable world shifts continually but evidently strongly nonlinearly from *Kaos* to *Kosmos*.

For some 13.8 billion years, the maximum-entropy chaos following the cosmic event known as the Big Bang has been yielding to order in the universal space-time field. The systems that order space and time are atoms, molecules, macromolecules, crystals, cells, systems of cells, and systems of systems of cells. On the cosmological scale, they are stars and stellar systems and galaxies and ultimately the cluster of galactic clusters: the metagalaxy.

The evolution of life, and the evolution of complex integral systems in general, is a complex ongoing response of the cosmos to the loss of coherence occasioned by the disruptive event known as the Big Bang.

The hypothesis assumes that the universe preexisted the Big Bang and that it regulates its own state. The import of coherence through the evolution of life and complexity compensates for the loss of coherence through the Big Bang and that it constitutes a means of the universe's self-regulation.

Holotropism is a manifest perceivable effect of the compensation of the loss of coherence and is an evolutionary phenomenon.

In subjective but entirely appropriate terms, the holotropic attractor can be defined as the yearning of all things in the universe for coherence. In this definition the holotropic attractor is an expression of a cosmic drive for wholeness.

It is the attraction to recover the coherence lost 13.8 billion years ago in the cosmic rupture we know as the Big Bang. This recovery is the essence and the ultimate purpose of the evolution that unfolds in state and time.

Evolution did not start with the Big Bang; it is not an arbitrary or even a special manifestation but the active expression of a trend rooted in a cosmic event. It is as real and its recognition as compelling as that of any event in the world.

Evolution is a continuous, nonlinear process without a beginning or an end. The increase of coherence through this process is the contribution of evolving systems and constitutes the net dean of direct concern to conscious beings, such as humans.

Implications for Meeting Our Sacred Quest

What does the new story of evolution mean for us—for our ability to respond to the call of our sacred quest?

Let us recall the basics. We are part—and a shining example—of a process that started with the Big Bang that has been structuring the universe ever since. It brought forth a plethora of complex and coherent systems, including us, multicellular organisms. The process continues. The universe is continually upshifting its initial state of *Kaos* toward the evolved state of *Kosmos*.

Evolution is a universal nonrandom process oriented toward the formation of complex and coherent systems. We are systems formed in this process. As this is a goal-guided and goal-oriented process and we are part of it, we are inherently adapted to aligning with it.

We are blessed with the endowments we need to meet and act on our sacred quest. We can recognize who we are and can discover how it is best for us relate to each other and to the planet. Yet we are constantly infringing the limits of the earth's sustainable boundaries. We are dancing *on* the planet but not dancing *with* the planet. We treat the planet as a passive backdrop to our dance, a mere supplier of the air, water, land, and other resources we need and claim as our possession. We are not treating Mother Earth as a valued partner in our dance.

Thinking that we can dance above and beyond the bounds and possibilities of the equilibrium is disturbed—we experience it in the changes of the climate and in the growing aridity of the land. Vast tracts are turning into desert. Hitherto habitable coastal areas are flooded, and entire islands are submerged by rising sea levels. In the polar regions, melting permafrost is emitting methane and other poisonous gases into the atmosphere. We are disrupting essential links among self-maintaining ecosystems and creating one-sided dependencies. We have reached the threshold of what could turn into the sixth mass extinction of life on earth.

We must urgently correct our steps and begin to dance consciously with the planet. We know what the planet can endure and how our actions affect it. We know how we could dance *with*, and not only *on*, our home planet.

Dancing with the planet is a dance we can master. We have the skills and the knowledge, the technologies and the information. We also have the support of the new story in the sciences. We now need to come up with the heartfelt commitment to dance *with* Mother Earth. This is humanity's, in practice *our*, sacred quest.

We are cosmic beings endowed with an articulate consciousness. We can apprehend our sacred quest, and we can act on it. We can embrace the universe's innate impetus toward wholeness and coherence and celebrate it in our own life.

We do not require a higher intelligence or any external authority to tell us how to live and what to do. Holotropism, the impetus toward integral wholeness in us and in our world, is encoded in our cells and is present in our consciousness. We need to raise it to our everyday awareness. Then we would join together and build the critical mass that will change the world.

We need to access and adopt humanity's sacred quest. It is *our* quest. No higher objective could we pursue in our life, and no greater service could we offer to the planet and the universe.

Holotropism is a fundamental property of the universe. Its consequence is a process that shifts the dominant character of physical reality from randomness and disorder to forms and levels of order. In terms of classical Greek cosmology, the observable world shifts continually but evidently strongly nonlinearly from *Kaos* to *Kosmos*.

Cosmic Love Language

The emerging universal truth is that love is the expression of the cosmic holotropism of all things that evolve in space and time. The evolution of the things that emerge in the universe is none other than the manifestation of the attraction toward oneness of the beings that came to grace our planet.

There is no more profound and important realization available to the conscious human being than the awakening to the truth that the universe is not a passive and indifferent background but the dynamic platform for the continued unfolding in us and around us of the striving to oneness encoded in all things. We are born into a dynamic, highly oriented universe that tends ineffably toward wholeness. The expression of this tendency is what we call universal and all penetrating love—in other words evolution in the cosmic perspective.

Holotropic attraction is as basic and as determinant of our movements and evolution through space and time as the known universal forces, but it is far more subtle in its effect. The manifestation of holotropism is an indication to align with the evolutionary impetus that underlines the evolution of every blade of grass and every unfolding of the constellations that emerge in the cosmos.

Becoming aware of the evolution induced by holotropism is the key to living and growing in our holotropic universe. Upon it hinges the evolution of humanity and the well-being of each and every individual human being.

The love inspired by holotropism expresses and communicates the yearning to recover by humanity some of the coherence it lost in the cosmic event we know as the Big Bang.

The post-Big Bang universe is in constant cosmically motivated and guided evolution toward wholeness. This evolution is expressed by perceived people as a yearning for universal coherence. We are children of a coherent, love-imbued universe. Ignoring this basic fact is the fundamental error that has shaped humanity's recent passage in space and time. It may not be too late to awaken to it.

To Remember

We are a part—and a shining example—of a process that started with the Big Bang and has been structuring the universe ever since. It brought forth a plethora of complex and coherent systems, including us, multicellular organisms. The process continues. Evolution is a universal, nonrandom process oriented toward the formation of complex and coherent systems. We are systems formed in this process. As this is a goal-guided and goal-oriented process and we are part of it, we are inherently adapted to aligning with it.

We have remarkable endowments: a conscious mind and the ability to know and govern the way we live and affect others around us. Our relatively evolved condition confers a responsibility on us. As the famous French saying has it: *noblesse oblige*. In our case, the obligation is a responsibility—the responsibility to live and grow in harmony with life on the planet. To align with the planet, we need an up-to-date comprehension of the world, and of ourselves and our role in the world. Then we could tackle the epochal tasks of meeting our responsibility and creating a more harmonious world.

These tasks are not to be taken lightly. Creating a harmonious, peaceful, and coherent world is not just a task we need to undertake, a task among others. It is a *quest*. Given the nature of this task, it is not an ordinary mission. It is a *sacred* quest. One that we need to undertake on behalf of humanity—as conscious and responsible members of the human family.

CHAPTER TWO

EVOLUTION: THE NEW STORY FROM SCIENCE

CHARLES EISENSTEIN

"Come, let us build a city and a tower whose top shall reach unto heaven."

Genesis 11:4

A strange malaise has overtaken our civilization. Its most evident expression is the decline of the West, but signs abound of its inexorable spread to all technologically developed societies. It drains our collective life of color and meaning, it puts even the most obvious solutions to our pressing ecological and social problems out of reach, it paralyzes us as we helplessly watch our descent into ruin.

The reason is that the sponsoring myth of civilization has dissolved—and we no longer can answer the deep questions of who we are and why we are here—and so we trundle forward under the habits of the myth that formed a generation or two ago.

Young people today do not remember the unbridled optimism, the can-do spirit, the sense of limitless horizons that molded the generation that came of age in the post-WWII era. In those days, belief in the myth of progress, the myth of ascent, the myth of dominion were nearly universal. Humanity was moving from one triumph to the next. One natural limit after another succumbed to our tools. We could travel at the speed of sound. We could communicate at the speed of light. We could raise new mountains and change the course of rivers. We could see to the farthest reaches of outer space and into the depths of the atom.

Very soon, it seemed, the age-old curses of disease and maybe even death would succumb as well. The destiny of humanity was to be free of all mortal limits. We were always on the brink of new marvels. "What will science think of next?" we wondered.

Soon as well, we thought, the burgeoning "social sciences"—political science, sociology, economics, psychology—would conquer our social problems just as engineers had conquered the material world.

Since those halcyon days of the middle twentieth century, science and technology have continued to progress, even to accelerate. Yet, the techno-scientific utopia everyone hoped for failed to materialize. Ever just a few more inventions away, it nonetheless remains where it always was—on the horizon.

One cannot say that life is categorically worse than it was in 1963. Neither, however, can one say it is better. By many metrics (life expectancy, infant mortality, racial equality, deaths by violence) life has improved; by others it has worsened. The prevalence of chronic disease has risen from five or 10 percent to at least 50 percent, and to these formerly rare conditions (e.g., autoimmunity, allergies, autism, obesity) medical science can offer little but palliation. Levels of depression, anxiety, and addiction are on a similar trajectory.

Our stalled progress, even our regress, toward a perfect technological utopia oddly mirrors the failure of science to achieve its own ambition of totality. Mirroring engineering's rapid progress toward the conquest of nature, in the decades following the Second World War, science seemed to be closing in on a Theory of Everything that would reduce all phenomena to one phenomenon, that would reduce quality to quantity, matter to number, and life to chance. Physics unified two of the fundamental forces of nature—electromagnetism and the weak force—into one in short order. Plausible grand unification theories incorporating the strong nuclear force soon followed. Surely gravity would not be far behind in a unification of all four forces in a Theory of Everything. In biology, too, the deciphering of the structure of DNA promised to lay bare the "blueprint of life," to reduce life to a set of instructions.

Science's rapid (apparent) progress toward the conceptualization of nature, and technology's rapid (apparent) progress toward the control of nature slowed, stalled, and in some sense has reversed since those heady times of the 1960s and 1970s. We have made tremendous progress in specific areas, delving, for example, into infinitesimal detail in the metabolic pathways of a cell. A metabolic graph displaying them would cover a vast wall in fine print. Yet somehow, none of that exact knowledge has helped us overcome the rising epidemic of chronic illnesses that involve dysfunctions of precisely these pathways. We see here a failure of the basic mythology of modernity.

We would like to believe that we moderns have transcended myth and superstition. Instead, we suppose, we derive our beliefs by applying pure reason to objective evidence, forming and testing hypotheses through the scientific method. Little do we see that the entire corpus of science is itself a highly elaborate mythology founded on little-questioned and unprovable metaphysical assumptions. Among them are the constancy of natural laws, the isolability of experimental variables, the repeatability of experiments, the independence of the experimenter (and his/her beliefs and intentions) from the outcome of the experiment, the absence of an ordering intelligence or consciousness inherent in matter, and finally that determinism and chance explain the fundamental workings of the universe.

This last item forms the creation myth of modernity. We live in a universe of ruthless chaos, against which we pit our own intelligence to carve out a temporary realm of order. Extending that order, imposing our intelligence onto a world that has none, domesticating the wild, insulating ourselves from (and harnessing and dominating) the impersonal, unconscious, purposeless forces of nature—that was the "sacred quest" of modernity. That is the myth—the myth called *progress*—that infused meaning and purpose into human affairs, that told us why we are here and what our destiny is.

That myth now lies around us in ruins. Without the myth of progress to animate our society, we grope and flounder. Sometimes we fall into nihilistic postmodernism (which is not "post" modern at all, but rather an attempt to come to grips with the meaninglessness of a universe of determinism and chance onto which we project meaning). Other times we try to revive the myth of progress, imagining that technological utopia is just around the corner, one or two new inventions away, that nanotechnology and genetic engineering and artificial intelligence will usher in the Age of Leisure, the perfected society, that the steam engine and AC power and the miracle of chemistry and atomic energy failed to bring. A few more stories on the Tower, and we will finally have reached the sky. But as the ecological and social failures of that ambition become harder to ignore, more and more we lapse into lassitude and despair.

A third response is to attempt to create a new story, a new sacred quest, a new mythology to animate our civilization. Already though, such a project still contains hidden seeds of the old story. It assumes that a myth is something humans create. As long as we believe that, a new story will seem empty, because after all, it is yet another projection of meaning onto a world that has none.

The new story we are looking for requires a much more radical change in our thinking. We must recognize that a myth is not something we just make up. It is woven into reality. To put it in somewhat paradoxical terms, in the new myth, a myth is not just a myth. We don't make it up. We discover it. We align with it. We inhabit it. And it inhabits us.

Let us draw an analogy to nonlinear thermodynamics. In any system with basic nonlinear features (like positive and negative feedback), order emerges spontaneously out of chaos—and not just order, but structure, organization, beauty. And because the most obvious embodiment of these qualities is life, we might say that the universe has an innate tendency toward life. This principle runs even deeper than physics; it is in mathematics too. One looks at the marvel of a fly grooming itself, or the graph of metabolic pathways of a cell, or a Mandelbrot set zoom video, and it seems that exquisite structure couldn't just happen that way, that an external agency must have designed it. But no. To resort to external agency is to comply with reductionist science's robbery of the sacred qualities of matter. Religion, despite its superficial opposition to science, has long been its accomplice. Science said, "*Matter is fundamentally absent in the qualities of design, purpose, organization, and beauty. They are but human projections onto determinism and chance.*" Religion agreed with the basic premise: "*Yes, matter by itself is absent in those qualities, but luckily we have God to add them in from the outside.*"

When we adopt a new story that understands the fundamental tendency of all things toward more complexity, more coherence, and more life, a new sense of purpose, a new sacred quest, is born within us. We no longer need to impose anything onto the world. We no longer need to conquer. We no longer need to dominate. Instead, we become participants in the cosmic process of unfoldment. We understand ourselves as agents and servants of the continued unfolding of life and beauty in the cosmos. We participate in the further coming alive of the world.

That is what human beings are for. Over four billion years of life's history on earth, the earth has become more and more alive. From prokaryotes to eukaryotes to multicellularity to angiosperms to the recent (one hundred million years) emergence of flowering plants, the biosphere has grown ever more complex, ever more diverse. Each new order, each new species, has contributed to that complexification. That is the purpose all life forms share in common. Humans are no exception. Gaia did not birth us, with all our unique gifts, by mistake. True, as a civilization we have not yet applied our gifts fully toward their true purpose. We have instead diminished life on earth, not increased it. And unless we align with a new story that recognizes the purpose we share in common with all life, we will continue to diminish it.

We will continue to diminish not just life in general, but our own lives as well. Another dimension of the new story is the principle of *interbeing*. We are not separate from the world. We are not separate from life. When a species goes extinct, when a forest is converted to a parking lot, something dies within us as well. Replacing intimate connections to nature and to communicate with technology-mediated substitutes, replacing participation with consumption, we become less alive. We become less *here*. The collapse of the old story, which takes the form of a crisis of separation, inevitably entails a psychological collapse as well.

Yet even this collapse that is bringing us to utter destitution is itself part of the process of the world coming more alive. We gaze upon the Tower, so tall, so consuming of life in its construction, and realize with dismay that the sky is just as far away as ever. Maybe we stop trying to take heaven by storm. Maybe we stop trying to attain the infinite through finite means. Maybe we realize that the sky begins an inch off the ground; therefore, we resolve to devote our genius as builders toward beauty rather than height.

In our destitution, something new is born that could come in no other way. The old story has to die before a new one can be born. Today, as Ervin Laszlo points us in chapter 1, a new story is emerging within us and among us, the story of a holotropic, wholeness-attracting and creating universe. A story of participation in a living, conscious universe that is intimately connected to us, in which our sacred quest is to contribute to the unfolding of life and beauty on earth.

That story has not come to save us from ourselves, however. Not even "collapse" will necessarily save us. We might choose instead to cling all the more tightly to the old story of separation and conquest. The new story of the coherence and wholeness-oriented universe will not necessarily rescue us. The new story does not command but merely beckons us. Are we ready to respond, will we embrace the new story and live up to our sacred quest?

CHAPTER THREE

THE COSMIC MEANING AND PURPOSE OF OUR SACRED QUEST

JUDE CURRIVAN

Our story is the story of our universe. As human beings, our own innate meaning is inseparable from the cosmic meaning that is embodied in its existential nature.

So, from the earliest times, wisdom teachings have shared narratives and communities have told stories that have sought to understand the world and our place and role within it.

In aiming to embrace and reconcile our inner and outer experiences, for millennia such narratives revered, as indigenous traditions continue to honor, the sanctity of an essentially living universe and its universal "web of life." By regarding the wholeness of creation as sacred, perceptions of right relationship extend to the whole of existence and, crucially, both seen and unseen realms.

In Europe, though, by the sixteenth century, the dominance and dogmatic views of the Catholic Church limited considerations and further investigations of what human existence means. Accordingly, reliance was imposed on superstition, rather than discoveries from explorations of the manifest world.

Yet, such discoveries were nonetheless being made.

Initially known as natural philosophers, pioneers including Copernicus who showed that our sun rather than earth is the center of our solar system, and Newton whose genius perceived the force of gravity and its being the same, whether causing an apple to fall from a tree, or sustain planets in their orbits, used observations and experimental measurements to provide the evidence for their insights. Indeed, it was the power of their methodical approach, instigated by Francis Bacon and leading to such revelatory knowing that resulted in later proponents of the method to be called scientists, derived from the Latin *scio*, meaning "to know."

For many of them, and continuing throughout the sixteenth and seventeenth centuries, their deeper aim was to reveal the divine as being embodied in the physical phenomena.

Yet, including Galileo held under house arrest for the rest of his life after providing further evidence in support of Copernicus, and Giordano Bruno burned at the stake for refusing to recant his views of the Cosmos, their being seen as encroaching on the prevailing views of the Church was highly dangerous.

Thus, a schism ensued and progressively grew, between exploration of the physical realm by scientists and its spiritual nature, being maintained as the sole remit of organized religion.

Untethered, except by the continuing spiritual beliefs of some of its advocates, throughout the eighteenth and nineteenth centuries, so-named modern science then proceeded as a merely secular means of exploring the world, and effectively devoid of any sense, acknowledgement of or interest in the sacred.

Increasingly, its successes enabled development of technologies that drove the Industrial Revolution and, with its materialistic and mechanistic worldview, hierarchies of governance and corporate structures, policies, and practices that have been perpetuated until now. Viewing the world as a complicated machine, whose workings can be separated and controlled, and using engineering terms to measure effectiveness, human beings and our planetary home came to be viewed as resources—cogs in managed and profit-driven endeavors.

The materialist perspective was continuing apace, when in 1858, Charles Darwin's and Alfred Russell Wallace's similar ideas of biological evolution proceeding through natural selection of organisms best fitted to their environments caused a furor in that it implicitly contested a belief in divine creation, despite neither researcher claiming so. By the later discovery of DNA, then RNA, and consequently the genetic code in the 1960s, a materialist worldview was so embedded that the incredible complexity of the workings of the genome was sidelined. Instead, a standpoint was taken that the evolution of organisms was driven by random and beneficent mutations of genes that then aligned with the processes of natural selection.

Even with the revolutionary scientific breakthroughs of quantum physics and relativity in the early twentieth century revealing that the mechanistic view of our universe was significantly flawed and calling for a philosophical reset, such a paradigm shift was marginalized. Rather, the radical insights of nonlocal connectivity and the need to view energy-matter as equivalent and space-time as invariant were harnessed for technological advances rather than harvested for wisdom.

The materialist perspective has also, yet without any proof, sought to maintain that somehow the immateriality of mind and consciousness arise from material brains. Consequentially, its ongoing view of a universe of inherent separation, essentially devoid of meaning and bereft of purpose, has also competitively and greedily driven overconsumption, environmental desecration, depletion and pollution, inequalities, and epidemic levels of stress and dysfunctional behaviors on personal, communal, and planetary levels.

Now, though, and actually enabled by its advanced technologies, radical discoveries, with scientific breakthroughs at all scales of existence and across numerous fields of research are turning its paradigm on its head—re-storying the sacredness of the whole world and remembering the cosmic meaning and further, the evolutionary purpose, of our sacred quest.

Converging with the tenets of Interspirituality and ancient and indigenous wisdom traditions, a cosmology is emerging of a living and nonlocally unified universe that meaningfully exists and purposefully evolves. Most fundamentally, it is asserting that mind and consciousness aren't something we have, but just what we are. What the whole world truly is. Therefore, reestablishing this innate reality is our sacred quest.

Wide-ranging evidence reveals that the appearance of our universe arises from deeper nonphysical realms of cosmic causation, as digitized and, vitally, meaningful in formation and pixelated at the most minute scale of existence, one the great pioneers of quantum physics.

In 2022, the Nobel Prize for Physics recognized the nature of its unified wholeness, or universal nonlocality, significantly acknowledging it as settled science. Derived from studies of black holes and extended to our entire universe is compelling evidence that its semblance of energy-matter and space-time manifests holographically.

In 2017, cosmological scale measurements of tiny temperature fluctuations in ancient radiation that fills the whole of space uncovered the characteristic fractal patterns of the so-named holographic principle. Also discovered throughout all smaller scales of existence—from vast clusters of galaxies to dynamics of solar systems, planetary-wide phenomena, to collective human behaviors down to the level of atomic particles—reveals a key attribute of the wholeness of a hologram, whether cosmic or human-made, to be reflected and nested throughout its constituent parts.

Coming into being some 13.8 billion years ago, our universe also embodies in its entirety a purposeful evolutionary impulse. The lowest entropic state of its miniscule, simplest, and yet exquisitely fine-tuned birth imbued it with an arrow of time. Ever since, it has undertaken, from past to present to future, an ongoing journey to ever greater complexity, individuated self-awareness, and coherent interdependence.

Rather than as a singular and implicitly chaotic big bang event, its tiny beginning, from which space has continued to expand, was the first moment of an essentially meaningful, purposeful, and continuing "Big Breath."

A reappraisal and expansion of the concept of entropy to that of in-tropy, as its universally meaningful in-formational content, is also enabling a deeper perception of its inherent purpose. From the first moment of the Big Breath, with the flow of time and expansion of space, universal in-tropy has inexorably increased, enabling a realization of its evolutionary journey to unfold and a new and unitive narrative to be told.

In addition to the existential meaning of our universe, a radical new understanding of its embodied evolutionary impulse is showing that meaningful in-formation underpins, pervades, and guides its universal emergence, and where too interdependent interactions predispose and presage further development.

Mere minutes after the Big Breath began, the matter of our universe coalesced as primordial nuclei of the simplest element, hydrogen, and the next simplest, helium. The abundance of helium, fixed so early, was likely crucial to enabling the synthesis from hydrogen and helium to more complex elements within stars forming hundreds of millions of years later. For without this initial profusion of helium included in the stellar mix, a key threshold fusing three helium nuclei to form carbon would have stalled. Unable to further progress, our universe would thus have been devoid of greater complexity and the eventual emergence of all carbon-based biological life, including ourselves.

Also, from a very early epoch, a cosmic web of electromagnetic fields came into being and stretched across the entirety of space. This, allied with gravity, organized the births of the first stars and crucially black holes to form swirling galaxies and vast galaxy clusters.

The subsequent lifecycles of successive generations of stars, fueled by nuclear fusion, synthesized heavier elements beyond carbon, to nitrogen, oxygen, and upward to iron. Beyond iron, however, the creation of still heavier and more complex elements, concluding with uranium, needed even more extreme conditions. Supernovae, deaths of the largest stars, and the maelstrom of massive stellar mergers, not only enabled their torrid conception, but also the explosive release of their entire elemental abundance to form immense interstellar clouds of stardust.

Replete too with molecular hydrogen and water ice, such clouds, shepherded by coherent magnetic fields and bathed by diffused ultraviolet light from nearby stars, provide intricate chemical laboratories for further complexity and act as harbingers of future planetary systems and biological lifeforms.

Their collaborative components and processes are being discovered to be extremely well optimized to enable the brewing of a varied range of complex carbon-based molecules, leading all the way to amino acids (the building blocks of proteins) and the threshold of organic life.

Laboratory simulations have revealed the strong likelihood that the nucleobases making up the DNA and RNA nucleic acid molecules that embed the genetic code also evolve in such clouds. There are only five of these, and for organic life to emerge, they then needed to combine with other types of molecules in an intricate and "in-formationally" guided dance to eventually form DNA and RNA.

Analysis of the effectiveness of DNA has shown that it is the best and one-in-a-million choice to guide biological emergence. So, the incredible intelligence and adaptability of this "five-letter" code is such that it has remained constant ever since and is exactly the same structure for all the subsequent profusion and evolutionary complexity of our planetary home, Gaia's, biosphere.

The final factor ensuring ideal conditions for the birth of planetary systems is the combined and optimal frequency and explosive power of supernovae. Interstellar molecular clouds form at the intersections of their shock waves, and successive pulses trigger their ordered gravitational collapse. If supernovae were more frequent and/or more powerful and/or closer, the clouds would be too turbulent; if less frequent and/or less powerful and/or further away, the clouds would disperse before planetary systems could form.

Ever-increasing evidence is showing that solar systems of central suns and encircling planets appear to be the norm for continuing the evolutionary arc of our universe. Indeed, so many have now been discovered that there are estimated to be significantly more planets than stars in our galaxy, and this is likely replicated in galaxies through our entire universe.

While interstellar clouds nurture our universe's evolutionary impulse to prebiotic complexity, in the intense cold of space, the energy needed for further emergence is absent. It is, thus, planetary homes, lit by their suns, that are vital for the subsequent emergence of biological life.

However, to do so requires planets or moons with suitable and stable gravitational fields, adequate and sustaining atmospheres, sufficient warmth, and, crucially, liquid water. Consequentially, the search for such exoplanets, beyond our own solar system, includes especial focus on rocky planets, such as ours, and optimally in what's known as habitable zones.

Around 4.6 billion years ago, in the depths of a gestating interstellar cloud, shock waves from a nearby supernova likely triggered such a collapse. It led to the birth of Gaia and the solar system—not as a chaotic in-fall but coherently into a protoplanetary disc with our young sun at its center and encircling protoplanets. As for earlier stages of the evolutionary impulse of our living universe, the innately in-formed interdependence of the entire system, after some early and itself enabling drama, settled into the precision and longevity of resonantly relational planetary orbits.

Provided with a cornucopia of elements, water, and prebiotic building blocks from her interstellar heritage, Gaia is wonderfully capable of nurturing the further evolution of complex biological life-forms. Ideally located in the habitable warm zone of our solar system, as a rocky planet (the densest in our planetary family and with a powerful and protective magnetic field), having a gravitational field able to retain a thick atmosphere and blessed with substantial water, she is a remarkable planetary Mother.

Over the last four billion years, not by passive continuity, but proactively by change and challenge, Gaia's emergence has not only survived but flourished. The collaborative cycles of her entirely interdependent *gaiasphere*, comprising rocks and minerals of her geosphere, waters of her hydrosphere, changing airs of her atmosphere, and ecosystems of her biosphere, have provided widely varied environments to sustain the evolutionary complexity and diversity of her organic children.

While still an investigative work-in-progress, there is growing evidence that rather than evolving in a linear sequence, interstellar cloud-sourced prebiotic building blocks, instead and at the earliest opportunity, converged as an optimal assemblage of organic potential. Utilized ever since and throughout the entire biosphere, they led to the emergence of protocell precursors to the earliest bacteria and archaea. Numerous examples of such "reticulate" evolution are now showing that dynamic, "in-formationally" imbued, and collaborative relationships within and between the organisms of Gaia's biosphere and the entire *gaiasphere*, enable their co-evolution as an organized and purposeful whole.

Underpinned by so-named holotropic attractors of meaningful in-formation, often and where feasible, evolutionary montages of preassembled organic components are being found to include different genetic lineages to optimize further emergence. Throughout Gaia's evolutionary journey, it seems that such coordination may have significantly aided the recovery and onward evolution of her biosphere after catastrophic breakdowns, by increasing survival and thrival chances and significantly scaling up and speeding up radical changes in speciation and diversity. These findings are progressing alongside a radical reappraisal of the nature and role of the genetic code itself.

The genome of a specific species of organism has a constant number of genes, acting as an in-formational library. Genes can be used, however, to code for multiple proteins offering wide-ranging functionality without needing to increase the genome itself. After a gene, or a part of it, has been transcribed from the genome, sections of its in-formational message are effectively genetically engineered. Spliced by being cut out or moved, the process results in a number of different protein variants, which are then also molecularly tagged to further alter and broaden their functions. So, the human genome of around twenty-two thousand genes, for example, codes for upward of four times as many proteins.

Vitally, while coding for the inherited characteristics and functions of an organism, the genome isn't just a read-only and thereby unchangeable instruction manual. Being responsive to ongoing, active, and potentially evolutionary in-formational processes within the entire organism and between an organism and its surroundings, it also has read-write capabilities to express its genes in different ways.

So, the genetic code isn't the controller of the organism but rather its servant. Indeed, if their genomes are removed, while then unable to replicate, repair damage, or undertake genome-linked adaptations, cells can still continue to convert food to energy and sustain all their coordination and communications—activities both within themselves and between each other.

The notion that organisms are machines created by their genes is thus fundamentally incorrect. Not only are genes not "selfish" in running the show of evolution, but neither organisms nor their genes are mechanistic and random accumulations of chemicals. Rather, biological organisms are meaningfully in-formed and individuated microcosms of our innately intelligent universe and an embodiment of its evolutionary impulse.

The reappraisal of the role of DNA and the genome has gone along with a (r)evolutionary overhaul of the so-named standard model of biological evolution. The model, known as Neo-Darwinism, is named after Charles Darwin's pioneering insights of evolutionary adaptation, updated to include the discovery of genetic inheritance. It assumes that based on the hereditary template of its genome, it is random mutations with presumed benefits that enhance the organism's fitness (adaptation) to its environment, and so over time—lots of time—gradually accomplish evolutionary progress.

Instead, discoveries are showing that alongside more dynamic roles of the genome, Neo-Darwinism's foundational presumption of beneficial random mutations being the primary driver of evolution, is fundamentally flawed.

Building from the emergence of prebiotic and the earliest organic lifeforms, substantial contingencies, redundancies, checks, balances, and corrections in the genetic replication processes to synthesize cellular structures have developed. These go to extraordinary lengths to reduce coding errors and so minimize the possibilities of random mutations. From an estimated error rate in human protein synthesis of one in ten thousand copies in transcribing the initial DNA instructions, further controls as the coding is transferred and then used by various types of RNA to construct the requisite proteins, improves the error rate to a miniscule one in more than a billion copies.

If random mutations were in any way helpful for evolution, let alone viewed as its primary driver, such massive efforts to prevent them would not be worthwhile in terms of the energy and effort that organisms undertake to prevent them.

Rather, an organism's highest priority is to sustain its coherence and integrity, while being open and able to purposefully, proactively, and beneficially adapt to evolutionary influences. The efforts to retain such integrity increase with individuated complexity. So, while single-celled organisms have very "fluid" genomes, sharing DNA to access multiple environmental niches, multicellular lifeforms progressively trade off and balance their bodily flexibility with their overall and ongoing viability.

The Neo-Darwinian model requires long lengths of time for other than minimal evolutionary changes, due both to its premise that mutations are random and additionally that they're only passively embodied through natural selection. Instead, there's ever more evidence that meaningful and intelligent in-formational processes and reticulate assemblages guide organic emergence and evolutionary complexity and can do so over much shorter time periods.

Furthermore and, indeed, as Darwin acknowledged toward the end of his life, there cannot be an understanding of such evolutionary processes while attempting to separate a biological entity from its environment. In complete contrast to the Neo-Darwinian model, entire ecosystems are being increasingly revealed to be in interdependent, co-evolutionary and dynamic partnerships, not only inclusive of their biological entities but also with the entirety of Gaia's *gaiasphere* and in even wider relationships with our sun and moon.

The misinterpreted Darwinian notion of "survival of the fittest" has also pictured constant conflict between organisms as being the main selector of their evolutionary fitness. While competition for environmental niches and resources do have their roles, it's rather cooperation and nested, or holarchic, organization that essentially drive evolutionary complexity. Collaborative relationships that are win-win, whether through competitive tensions or cooperative, mutuality supported the earliest emergence of organic evolution and have continued to do so ever since.

Such cooperation is innately founded on a felt sense of relationships. Alongside and beyond the evolution of self-aware intellect, Gaia has progressively nurtured empathy and emotional attachments. In the mutually supportive and loving relationships of mates, parents and offspring, and families and communities, are embedded circles of caring. Bacteria, insects, and fish work together to look after others of their communities, especially the vulnerable. And in the altruism of rats and monkeys, the grieving of elephants not only for their own kin but for a human caretaker, the self-sacrifice of a human stranger, and the protection of other species by humpback whales from orcas, the circles of care further expand and evolve as spirals of compassion.

In this book, Ervin Laszlo has posed the issue. Keeping us living and evolving can be, and is, a meaningful quest, because we are not here by chance. There is a reason—a sacred reason—for our existence. We should come back to the perennial philosophical query: Why is humankind on earth?

In affirming that, "in a spiritual context, humanity's purpose for existence is to follow the guidance and achieve the will of a higher spirit or consciousness," Laszlo notes that, "the purpose of human existence can also be provided by science."

Here, I have shared how scientific breakthroughs and evidence are indeed converging with the unitive tenets of Interspirituality to tell what Ervin has elsewhere called, "Perhaps the greatest story ever told—now told with the authority of cutting-edge science."

These discoveries are not only probing the deeper "how" of our existential being, currently the sole aim of the scientific method, but also, in doing so, unavoidably respond to a reason for "why." In doing so, they are finally bringing to fruition the revelatory aims of the scientific pioneers of the sixteenth and seventeenth centuries—by revealing that the how and the why of our existence are inextricably combined.

They tell of a living and loving universe that meaningfully exists to purposefully evolve as a unitive entity. This is its, and thus our (as its microcosmic co-creators), sacred cosmic meaning and purpose. As its ongoing Big Breath breathes through us in every moment, our sacred quest is both vast and intimate.

By individually and collectively remembering that we are inseparable from each other, Gaia, and the whole world, it seems to me that our universe is inviting us, as family members of its wondrous and vast communities of life, to awaken to our sacred quest, to become their co-evolutionary partners and take our next steps into the emergent adventure of shifting toward a world that is coherent and whole.

CHAPTER FOUR

THE SACRED QUEST AND OUR QUEST FOR A UNIVERSAL SPIRITUALITY

ROBERT ATKINSON

The "sacred" has always been a special, distinguished designation. This opportunity to explore, identify, and carry out our sacred quest offered to us by Ervin Laszlo comes at just the right time. What the world needs now is to upshift its consciousness toward the sacredness of collective unity and wholeness.

Not only does humanity have a sacred quest, but we each also have our own individual sacred quest, however we discover, define, and carry that out for ourselves. Both are essential to the other. As we each carry out our individual sacred quest, the collective quest becomes fulfilled. This is when we will experience our greatest success in life, knowing that our personal sacred quest is helping carry out humanity's collective sacred quest.

A most important consideration is what exactly gets this designation of "sacred." In a classic context, *some things* are set apart as holy and consecrated, while in a more indigenous and increasingly universal context, *all things* can be cherished, revered, venerated, and held in the highest regard as being essential, interconnected components of a "sacred" creation.

What bridges these two ways of understanding "sacred" is remembering that unity, harmony, and wholeness is the nature of creation. The entire universe is a wholeness-in-motion. Our sacred quest might even be to recreate and reflect that innate unity and wholeness of all things around us.

Most needed now, in our divisive times, is recognizing and appreciating all things as tied together in a sacred web of wholeness, the entirety of which is to be revered and cherished.

This big-picture, holistic context for this theme is approached here from an interspiritual perspective, focusing on the upshift in consciousness we are witnessing now. This has been a long time coming; it is the culmination of a long evolutionary process.

Toward a Universal Spirituality

As we irresistibly move toward greater and greater levels of cooperation, collaboration, and unity, we are also moving closer to the fullest expression of our innate wholeness.

This is exactly what Brother Wayne Teasdale recognized at the turn of this millennium. He characterized this shift in consciousness as bringing about:

> an interdependence of all spiritual traditions;
> a new, interconnected universal civilization;
> an ecological awareness of the fragility of the earth; and
> an emerging unitive consciousness available to all.

He said this shift comes "from the heart of all mysticisms." This points to what Teilhard de Chardin referred to as "a single energy at play in the world." We are at a watershed moment in humanity's progress toward fulfilling its sacred quest.

All sacred traditions are within this single evolutionary flow, reflecting a unitive force impelling humanity toward its destiny. In our time, a universal spirituality is emerging, bringing humanity within reach of its sacred quest.

Through periodic leaps of consciousness, each sacred tradition has contributed a unique quality in this unfolding process of humanity's spiritual heritage. In *The Essential Mystics*, Andrew Harvey identified these interrelated "ways of approaching the unfathomable mystery" as:

> from the First Peoples traditions, *the way of reverent intimacy with nature*, being humble before the majesty of the universe;
> from ancient Greek mysticism, *the way of beauty*, sensing deeply the splendor of the world;
> from Hinduism, *the way of presence*, being in pure awareness of the indivisibility of all things;
> from Judaism, *the way of holiness*, seeing the divine as pervading human life;
> from Taoism, *the way of the Tao*, living in unimpeded harmony with all things;
> from Buddhism, *the way of clarity*, waking up to the pure freedom of unconditional compassion in the world;

- from Christianity, *the way of love in action*, becoming transformed to reflect the Creator's unwavering love for the entire creation; and
- from Islam, *the way of passion*, knowing the peace that comes in surrendering one's entire being to the Unknowable.

Out of Division, emerges *the Way of Unity*

Following these, in the mid-nineteenth century, out of the division, discord, and inequality of Persia, Bahá'u'lláh similarly renewed the spiritual verities by identifying *the way of unity* as the means of healing the ills of an ailing humanity.

This primary principle is vividly expressed in his statement, "The well-being of humankind, its peace and security, are unattainable unless and until its unity is firmly established."

This mid-nineteenth century refocusing of spiritual values was followed by advances in all realms of human rights, from the end of slavery to women's rights, to the first convening of the world's religions, to the long struggle for civil rights, and beyond.

With these advances, humanity is approaching a time promised by the sacred traditions, when humanity will restore the world to wholeness, bringing about a new earth by establishing unity, harmony, and coherence on a global scale.

However, this long-awaited future depends upon the continued convergence of science and spirituality because they are halves of the same whole, complementary perspectives on the same reality. They both help us to:

> understand the mysteries of our universe;
> identify the single force guiding evolution; and
> live in harmony with all things.

Both science and spirituality are leading humanity toward the fulfillment of its sacred quest by making clearer how all the parts comprise an undivided wholeness in which cooperation maintains the coherence and well-being of the whole.

This is an unprecedented moment in history, when science has uncovered evidence of nonlocality and entanglement, confirming what spiritual traditions have said for centuries: the entire creation is the fullest embodiment of wholeness. Science and spirituality converge on the biggest questions of existence, both giving humanity a common sacred quest.

Science and spirituality also converge in understanding unitive consciousness as the organizing principle upon which the entire universe was formed and still guides its ongoing evolution. Unitive consciousness-in-action is when our work in the world becomes one with that wholeness-in-motion all around us.

Because evolution—and history—do not occur in a straight line but rather in a nonlinear, spiral-like process, divisions and separation persist even as a universal spirituality is emerging to recreate the oneness of all things. The very nature of evolution, which is cyclical, expansive, and inclusive, supports a universal spirituality that is leading the way to humanity's next stage of its collective enfolding.

The Emerging Unitive Age

A holistic, unitive view of evolution recognizes the primary role of cyclical progress, by which each cycle brings about an expansion of unity beyond existing circles of unity to create new, larger, and more inclusive circles of unity until all circles of unity eventually merge into one. This view of social evolution as expansive, inclusive, and unifying at the same time was first agreed upon by both science and spirituality in the mid-to-late nineteenth century.

Beginning in 1852, the writings of Bahá'u'lláh signaled a leap in humanity's consciousness that moved beyond the prevailing nationalistic perspective to introduce the primary principle of the oneness of humanity.

He said, "The earth is but one country and mankind its citizens … Ye are the fruits of one tree, and the leaves of one branch … So powerful is the light of unity that it can illuminate the whole earth."

The Baha'i writings go on to explain a cosmology that verifies the latest quantum discoveries: "This endless universe is like the human body … all its parts are connected one with another … linked together in the utmost perfection."

Abdu'l-Baha, son of Bahá'u'lláh, made this concept of progressive evolution even clearer: "The evolution of existence is one; the divine order is one. All beings great and small are subject to one law and one order."

This is a fully developed view of evolution in which all things are interconnected and equally dependent upon the same Creator. Thus, evolution is purposeful, progressive, and it is leading to larger and larger circles of cooperation.

In 1871, the lesser known side of Charles Darwin also acknowledged this view of evolution in his pioneering understanding of social evolution as a process of unfolding and expanding circles of unity when he said in *The Descent of Man*: "As man advances in civilization, and small tribes are united into larger communities, the simplest reason would tell each individual that he ought to extend his social instincts and sympathies to all members of the same nation, though personally unknown to him. This point being once reached, there is only an artificial barrier to prevent his sympathies extending to the men of all nations and races."

Darwin expresses here the principle of collective altruism, or the universal Golden Rule writ large. In one sweeping notion, he takes the natural law of cooperation from the individual level to the global level. With this evolutionary trajectory—which is not without its ups and downs—the next stage in humanity's collective evolution would be the realization of another universal spiritual principle, that of peace on earth.

This underlying harmony of science and spirituality on the direction of social evolution illustrates that cooperation is destined to prevail on greater and greater levels, culminating in world unity, which is why we designate this the coming of the Unitive Age.

Responding to Humanity's Sacred Quest

This book shows how science and spirituality, particularly interspirituality, are in harmony through their agreement that we exist in a unified wholeness-in-motion of the entire creation around us. It also shows why they agree on our purpose, or sacred quest, as being, similarly, one of serving this wholeness to bring about the merging of our changing realm of existence with its source, the changeless realm that has brought all things into existence and is guiding us toward this re-union. This would complete and fulfill the super-coherence of which we and all created things in the universe are integral and intricate parts.

What is needed now is the universal recognition that there is a quest to be fulfilled in the flow and unfolding of evolution to ensure that the enfoldment of all parts into one unified wholeness-in-motion occurs before it is too late.

Our sacred quest, in whatever way we are each capable of, is to be a protagonist in the story not only of the oneness and wholeness of humanity, but also the story of the oneness and wholeness of creation. This would be a unitive narrative harmonizing cutting-edge science with an age-old spiritual vision of peace on earth.

We are living in a spiritual springtime, with new unitive principles and collaborative ways of being slowly but deliberately emerging that will fulfill the destiny of a fully integrated, compassionate, and loving humanity.

This is the way of unity, reclaiming a unitive consciousness and applying unitive principles on all levels simultaneously:

> to find inner peace by personally aligning with the transformative forces of the evolutionary impulse through our own focused spiritual practice;
>
> to build interpersonal peace by becoming a source of social good and contributing to strong and unified communities; and
>
> to build world peace by contributing to the renewal of the social, national, and global infrastructures of an ever-advancing civilization.

The way of unity is designed to build a greater strength and fullness of unity-in-diversity on its way toward peace. This great new era that will unfold over the coming decades and centuries is the time foretold by all the world's sacred traditions when a unitive consciousness will become the norm.

This is what it will take to make it possible for the equality of women and men to be realized, for a balance between the extremes of wealth and poverty to be realized, for freedom from all forms of prejudice to be realized, for harmony between science and spirituality to be realized, and for the protection of nature as a divine trust to be realized, all preeminent unitive principles of our time.

This is also the time when narratives will become unitive, when justice will become unitive, when economics will become unitive, when education will become unitive, when all forms of media will become unitive, when relationships on all levels of society will become unitive, and when local, state, national, and global governance will become unitive. This is the time when all our relationships and initiatives on all levels will be carried out for the express purpose of bringing about and maintaining unity.

When all these interdependent prerequisite stepping-stones have been crossed, the unity of the human family will be possible. This will complete the preconditions for what the Unitive Age—and our sacred quest—is ultimately leading to, the time when peace will prevail on earth.

The way of unity is integral to our return to an undivided wholeness that is the nature of creation. The reason we exist, the goal toward which we evolve, is the realization of our unity. When we become the living, embodied reflection of the sacred unity around us, we will see the fulfillment of humanity's sacred quest.

This is achieved by living with a unitive consciousness, where unity is all there is. In this consciousness, we are connected on a deep level with all other things. Achieving a unitive consciousness is also humanity's sacred quest.

Our call to action is initiating and guiding the spiritual regeneration of ourselves, our communities, our institutions, and our social structures on all levels so that the human family and all creatures on the planet can live together as a vast, all-inclusive web of wholeness-in-motion.

There is no other way to build unified communities and create a peaceful world than by each circle of unity adopting and living by unitive principles facilitating the fullness, inclusivity, and belonging that will culminate in the unity of the entire human family and the eventual merging of all circles of unity into one unified circle of wholeness, in which there will be no one left to exclude.

No greater, more sacred, quest is there than to become the cause of peace and well-being in the world. As the great spiritual traditions affirm, love is a universal, timeless elixir, the supreme force through which we can fulfill humanity's sacred quest: achieving wholeness and coherence on earth.

CHAPTER FIVE

Our Sacred Quest in the Historical Perspective

Ignazio Masulli

The first scientific revolution, founded on the physics of Galileo and Newton and integrated by the philosophy of Bacon and Descartes, long supported an alienating conception of the relationship between man and nature. Indeed, it attributed the source of knowledge to an abstract human subject, placed above and outside the world, which was conceived as a mere object of that knowledge.

This epistemological conception did not take long to be reflected in a more general paradigm of man's domination over nature and over other men, largely influencing the social organization and behaviors in the following centuries.

In the final analysis, it is to this fundamental contradiction that we must trace the concept of the claim of superiority and omnipotence of human activity. And this concept ended up causing the major imbalances that afflict the contemporary world to the point of reaching limits that are no longer sustainable.

The Imbalances of the Contemporary World

The first of the aforementioned imbalances is constituted by the serious damage caused by environmental pollution and climate warming, which threaten the continued existence of the species.

In fact, the warming of the planet's surface is mostly due to the accumulation in the atmosphere of greenhouse gases that are produced by human activities.

In 2020 their production—which has continued to grow since the industrial revolution—marked a new peak in the strong acceleration that has occurred since 1980.

These constantly growing trends explain the fact that in 2022 we exceeded an average increase in temperatures of 1.15 degrees Celsius compared to pre-industrial levels, and we are close to the limit of 1.5 degrees Celsius, which we promised ourselves not to exceed in the agreements signed at the United Nations Paris Conference in December 2015.

Already, with a global temperature increase of 1.1 degrees Celsius, unprecedented changes in the earth's climate are occurring in every region of the world: rising sea levels, extreme weather events, and rapid disappearance of frozen sea surfaces. Further warming will increase the magnitude of these changes. Every 0.5 degree Celsius increase in global temperature will cause increases in the frequency and severity of heat spikes accompanied by extraordinarily heavy precipitation and drought in many regions. According to the latest International Plant Protection Convention report, adverse climate impacts are already more extreme and far-reaching than expected and are likely to seriously affect the living conditions of a large part of the world's population.

The second imbalance is constituted by the "scissors" widening of the economic-social inequalities between the richest countries in the north of the world and the poorest ones in the south, as well as within both the former and the latter.

It depends on the relationship between development and underdevelopment. The "scissors" movement of this increasing gap shows that here we do not have a simple dualism, but a precise relationship. The underdevelopment of the more backward countries is not merely a matter of delay.

The fact is that the reasons behind underdevelopment have to do with the very ways in which growth has been achieved in the advanced countries.

Moreover, it is quite clear that the problems of underdevelopment, in turn, have repercussions for the stronger economies in a regime of the international economic system is increasingly subject to cycles of interdependence.

The most rigorous studies indicate that the richest 10 percent of the world's population receives 52 percent of total income, while the poorest half of the world's population earns 8.5 percent of it. If we consider the data relating to overall wealth, the inequalities are even more pronounced. In fact, the poorest half of the world's population practically has no income, since they own just 2 percent of the total, while 76 percent of the total income belongs to the 10 percent of the richest.

Also inextricably linked to the other two is the growing **demographic imbalance** between the populations living in the north and south of the world. This imbalance is all the more worrying if it is considered in the context of the forecasts regarding the exponential growth of the world population.

The first element is given by the growing aging of the population in the richest countries, especially in the United States of America and Western Europe. This demographic decline corresponds to an opposite trend in many countries in the south of the world, that is to say in those that have not yet broken the vicious circle between greater poverty and greater population.

It follows that of the total increase of two billion people expected by 2050, 52 percent will live in sub-Saharan Africa and 25 percent in central and southern Asia. The inhabitants of North Africa and Western Asia will also continue to grow, but more slowly. While in Europe and North America the population will grow by only 2 percent. By 2050, the population of sub-Saharan Africa will more than double (2.2 times the current one).

It should also be underlined that the ten countries south of the Sahara in which the greatest increase in inhabitants will have to bear the burden of 34 percent of the increase in the world population alone. And these are countries whose gross domestic product (GDP) per capita, made comparable at purchasing power parity, varies between 475 and 6.576 dollars a year. While that of the nine richest countries in the European Union, plus the USA, ranges from 37.140 to 80.060 dollars.

With the result that the GDP per capita of the richest countries will continue to grow in a multiplicative manner, while it will decrease enormously in the poorest countries, precisely due to the extraordinary increase in inhabitants among whom that GDP, already very reduced, will have to be shared.

All of this demonstrates the inexorability of the noose created by the fact that greater poverty leads to greater population and vice versa.

It is precisely the overcoming of this equation that allowed the most developed countries of the Euro-Atlantic area to complete, during the nineteenth and early twentieth centuries, the demographic transition that allowed them to escape from this spiral.

Over and above the figures themselves, the chief point is the population explosion. Given the present system of economic and political relations, its incompatibility with the limits of employment and exploitation of resources appears quite insoluble.

As we have seen, these are imbalances that are closely interconnected with each other. Their global dimensions loom increasingly threatening over the evolution of our species, but also, in more or less direct ways, over that of other living species.

The question to ask ourselves, then, is whether and how we will be able to overcome these imbalances to ensure that we and the other living beings on earth have an evolution free from pitfalls and open to a better future.

In order to undertake a completely different perspective, it is necessary to definitively free ourselves from the old epistemological paradigm.

This is not only possible, but it is also necessary due to the profound changes introduced by the second scientific revolution in the way of understanding evolution.

The Turning Point: The Second Scientific Revolution

The change of perspective indicated by the second scientific revolution is the product of a new development in biological, psychological, cognitive, and systems sciences. Their results have increasingly contributed to redefining the nature and source of knowledge, along the lines of a "natural epistemology."

Knowledge is no longer attributed to an abstract subject outside nature, which is conceived as a mere object of knowledge. Cognitive activity is an integral part of the evolutionary process and proceeds together with it at various degrees of evolution.

In this perspective, the traditional reference to a self-centered and all-knowing subject whose cognitive capacity suffers no limitations or conditionings no longer holds. Such a subject would be alien from the world that it nevertheless tried to describe.

What traditional epistemology had cut out is reintroduced; that is, the real, historical procedures of knowledge, ultimately its own "factory" is brought into existence; and thus, we can see how the subject of knowledge was concealed till then, expelled from the world, estranged from it.

The subject is finally made to belong to the world once more: its description of the world becomes its description of itself as it describes the world.

In the 1970s and 1980s, this turning point was brought about by the most significant results in evolutionary biology, cognitive science, as well as in the study of complex systems.

These results provide us with all the elements to affirm that knowledge takes place alongside that of natural processes of evolution and that the transcendence it entails is posed by evolutionary growth itself.

After all, the fully organic character of the nature-knowledge nexus is reaffirmed—which means nothing less than that knowledge is fully reinscribed within natural evolution.

In short, we find ourselves before a nature that, in evolving, knows itself and of which our own knowledge is itself an integral part.

In other words, the cognitive process does not lie outside or over against nature as being referred to as a knowing subject; nor does it exclude from itself, or distinguish as alien, nature as an object of knowledge, a mere passive or residual datum.

We can no longer deal with knowledge in extrinsic terms of reference, nor in terms of subject and object, such as would bar it off from the evolutionary process. The cognitive process and the evolutionary process move together as one.

The overthrow of the old paradigm is also important, and not secondarily, to free man from the other abstract and alienating conception that justified his position of dominion over other men, in a society that is also reified and reduced to a mere object, like nature.

From a consciousness of evolution to conscious evolution, we are required to make an unprecedented leap. This cannot be achieved without moving onto a new plane of consciousness: we are called upon to evolve a historical awareness of ourselves as a species. Today the very problem of life and the perpetuation of life is a problem of historical choices.

No longer is the responsibility for evolution entrusted to the instinctive defense mechanisms with which the individual is endowed, and which constitute the almost exclusive source of our present value judgments. Today this responsibility is a problem that appears in terms of historical decisions involving the entire species.

Knowing as we do how insufficient the equilibrium that has been achieved with respect to the historical utilization of the forces of production is, we are obliged to envisage a more profound equilibrium, to be achieved at the level of conscious regulation. This necessity to move toward conscious regulation becomes a factor in the crisis of contemporary society.

Awareness of our unstable equilibrium of our dance on the planet, of our irrational appropriation of nature, of the disturbance of harmony and the need to restore that harmony, all this means an objective sacred quest to assure the survival of our species. The problem thus appears in terms of historical choices regarding the whole of humanity.

Taking up such a challenge requires the ability to recognize our most authentic needs and to reestablish the ultimate goals of our evolution and that of other living species.

The inadequacy of the social cognitive maps on the basis of which we have hitherto been able to think and act, can only be overcome by clear-headed analysis.

The difficult leap to make is precisely that of pushing ourselves beyond the cognitive maps we have available and within whose boundaries we are used to thinking and acting.

In reality, the problems demonstrate how human beings, by virtue of being able to exercise learned behavior and possessing individual will, are able to behave in ways that are anti-evolution as well as pro-evolution. Systems of values as factors of control and regulation, operating in a seemingly intuitive way, can guide man toward survival or detour him from it.

We can add that, similarly to what has occurred in relationships with nature, also in relation to their own social construction, men have reacted by mainly pursuing presumptions of supremacy and power. This led to the prevalence of attitudes of domination and antagonism.

From this point of view, too, it looks as if the value systems and behavior patterns that characterized the dominant cognitive maps of the previous centuries will have to be replaced by others more suited to a new path of history and evolution.

As regards both external and internal environments, the transformations of contemporary society pose basic problems that cannot be tackled, let alone solved, without a clear awareness of the historical limits of our modes of thought and action; not without a critique of the type of rationality that has characterized the history of social organization and the crisis with which we must now come to terms.

Historical rationality developed in terms of domination and antagonism suffers from all its limitations, which are therefore the subjective limits of contemporary man, of his partiality and impotence.

So that the subjects in whose fallacious interest that rationality had also affirmed the subjugation and objectification of nature, as well as the disciplining and reification of society, found themselves, in the end, so oppressed and objectified with respect to themselves that they were incapable of getting away from their alienation.

As long as their efforts at emancipation continue to be guided by that same type of rationality, they cannot help but turn into their opposite: in the consolidation of the illusory context of which they are prisoners.

At this point, we need a consciousness of our human condition so profound as to be capable of changing it through a conscious choice of our objectives as a species. In other words, we need a great leap forward in overcoming the current limits of the way of thinking about our evolution. Only such a leap can enable us to build a new paradigm to oppose that which has led us to the dead-end crisis and closed possible future prospects of our ability to choose. A paradigm that must be the expression of new cognitive maps bearing new value systems, social models, collective behaviors.

Today, if we want to face and attempt to overcome the great imbalances that risk compromising the evolution of our species and that of other living species on earth, it is necessary to take another great leap forward. It must consist in *the passage from the consciousness of evolution to conscious evolution.* This means becoming capable of consciously choosing and pursuing the necessary and desirable objectives for the future evolution of all life on the planet.

The Urgency of Our Sacred Quest

This is the challenge we face and what we must take up. In order to succeed, we need to reach a new and deeper level of our consciousness: the consciousness of being an integral part of nature and of a whole to which we belong by virtue of a constitutive and indissoluble bond.

Ultimately, we must reach an even deeper level of consciousness, one that goes beyond the limits of our own existence and that allows us to feel part of a whole that includes and exceeds us.

This requires us to enter even deeper into our own being and broaden our perceptions. In this way we will be able to fully understand the evolution we are part of and become bearers of the sacred quest of safeguarding the evolution of life on earth.

CHAPTER SIX

DREAM THE SACRED DREAM: THE AMERICAN WISDOM TRADITIONS AND THE SACRED QUEST OF CONTEMPORARY HUMANITY

Alberto Villoldo

The ancient wisdom keepers of the Americas know and serve a sacred dream, one that they believe guides planets across the heavens and our destinies here on earth. The sacred dream is a map to the future of humanity and all creatures on the earth, but it has no paths you can follow and no trails other than the ones you blaze yourself. It is ephemeral, changing every instant, surprising you at every turn, as in a dream.

Ancient Americans had no writing, so they had to commit their legends and everyday knowledge—from making fishhooks to building pyramids—to memory. These were stories then told around the campfire by one generation to the next. But even more important than how to make fire were the teachings for serving the sacred dream, for it contained the codes for the implicate order of the universe. It allowed them to understand the seasons, how the bees pollinate the flowers, and how all living beings are connected and related to each other.

All My Relations

With this knowledge, the ancient sages bred and crossbred their wisdom and their corn to create more than four hundred varieties of maize; they gazed at the night sky and forecast eclipses decades into the future. Meaning and purpose arose naturally in their hearts because they knew they were part of a great plan. They knew that the sacred dream had to be held and served by everyone, or it would quickly turn into a collective nightmare.

Every living cell in our body obeys this same dream, keeping the well-being of the body before their personal one. When some cells choose to survive at the expense of the entire body, we call them cancer. Sadly, today humans are more worried about our personal comfort than the well-being of the earth. We are making the planet sick and committing a kind of matricide, endangering the life of our own Mother Earth.

The men and women who serve the sacred dream are still today known as EarthKeepers. They have no enemies in this world or the next. Their resources are vast. Noncausal events are common in their lives, and they can be the product of the future and not only of their past or even their genes. Synchronicity and serendipity become commonplace in their lives, and they are masters of the journey beyond death into infinity.

When we become aware of the sacred dream, we recognize that the universe is not made only of dead rocks hurling through space, of lifeless energy, or of the dark matter of science. Instead, we understand that the cosmos is pulsing and conscious, longing to create life and beauty, birthing blue-green planets, spiral galaxies, and more than twenty thousand species of butterfly on our earth.

Each one of us has been given for safekeeping a fragment of the sacred dream to express in our own way. When we forget that we carry an essential and necessary piece of the dream, our lives begin to spiral into disarray, our personal lives turn into nightmares, and our world descends into chaos.

Many of us have exchanged the sacred dream for a dream of personal fame and fortune, of power, or of wealth. Meanwhile today's global crises—from climate change to species extinction to war, famine, and disease—are calling us to find a new dream for humanity. They are inviting us to wake up from the slumber we are in so that all the possibilities of the future become available to us, and we may together dream a new world into being. Not a new earth, our beautiful planet. But a new humanity, that what the prophecies of the Americas call the dawn of *homo Luminous*, humans that are stewards of all life on the planet. This is the essence of the sacred quest discussed in this book.

When you find you follow the sacred quest and dream the sacred dream, the creative power of the universe becomes available to you to create beauty in your life first, and then in the world. You live fearlessly, you discover the answer to "Who am I?" "Where do I come from?" and "Where am I going?"

Like the sages of the Americas, you can become an EarthKeeper. You can dare to speak the inconvenient truths, uphold universal values that honor all life, and perform daily acts of courage. Your choices and lifestyle will help you to forge a sacred dream for yourself. They will help you craft a destiny infused with courage and driven by vision. EarthKeepers are essential today when dreaming happens only when we sleep, where cowardice is honorable, where hindsight seems wise, where truth is uncommon, and where spirituality is spineless.

In the sacred dream, the real nature of water is light, the nature of earth is light, of fire is light, and of wind is light. As your consciousness explores the sacred dream, you realize that even the planets, the sun, the trees, and the whales are made of light wrapped tightly into matter.

Light is the primordial "stuff" of the universe. The Primordial Light was known to the Andean sages as *Ti*. Its birthplace was Lake Titicaca. And the legends say that this light is shining brightly again onto EarthKeepers everywhere to help us follow the sacred quest and newly dream the world into being.

CHAPTER SEVEN

OUR SACRED QUEST IN THE VISION OF SPIRITUAL MASTER PETER DEUNOV

DAVID LORIMER

We look forward to the time when the power to love will replace the love of power. Then will our world know the blessings of peace.
— William Ewart Gladstone,
British Prime Minister

In chapter 1, Ervin Laszlo writes, "There is no more profound and important realization available to the conscious human being than the awakening to the truth that the universe is not a passive and indifferent background but the dynamic platform for the continued unfolding in us and around us of the striving to oneness encoded in all things." The inherent dynamic of evolution in terms of what he calls a holotropic attractor as a drive toward wholeness is itself a magnet for coherence, especially when we recognize the oneness of life and mind.

This brings to mind Teilhard de Chardin's vision of the law of love being embedded in every element of nature where "God's evolutionary vision of the world is that we will all one day come to love one another. In this great union of love, we will truly recognize who we were meant to be, we will realize that love is the only way to personal and universal fulfilment. Our task and purpose is therefore to learn to love, based on understanding of love as a universal cosmic force that binds the universe together."

In this chapter, I articulate the vision of the Bulgarian sage Beinsa Douno (Peter Deunov 1864–1944) of the coming Culture of Love as a sacred quest that truly realizes our spiritual capacities and potential. The fundamental principles of his teaching are Divine Love, Divine Wisdom, and Divine Truth, which we all must know, study, and apply. Deunov writes:

The first principle on which the whole of existence is based is Love; it brings the impulse to life; it is the compass, the stimulus within the human soul.

The second principle is Wisdom, which brings knowledge and light to the mind, thus enabling human beings to use the forces of Nature in a noetic [higher reason and insight] way.

The third principle is Truth; free the human soul from bondage and encourages us to learn, work well and make efforts towards self-sacrifice.

There is nothing greater than these principles; there is no straight up for sure path.

In these three principles lies the salvation of the world!

Love eliminates hatred, violence, murder, war.

Wisdom eliminates ignorance, error, darkness.

Truth eliminates lies, slavery, sin.

The important point here is the emphasis on fundamental divine principles rather than on ideas and beliefs. Such principles are universal, even if refracted through different cultures and spiritual traditions to take particular forms. To these he adds the two further supporting principles of equity or justice, and virtue or goodness. Together, these form a pentagram representing the cosmic human and the path of the aspiring disciple. He explains: "Love brings life, wisdom brings light and knowledge, while truth brings freedom. Love is fundamental to life, while light, knowledge, and freedom are conditions for the manifestation of love."

This symbol of the pentagram is also danced and enacted in the third part of the sacred dance movements of paneurhythmy created by Deunov, who also composed the music. You can see videos on YouTube of these movements being performed in the high Rila mountains in the Seven Lakes region. With the musicians in the center and the dancers in concentric circles, paneurhythmy (literally universal harmony of movement) represents dynamic coherence and interconnectedness with the vertical dimensions of Spirit and Earth, and horizontally between the dancers. It is a beautiful—even sublime—feeling to come together in this larger whole where individual polarities representing masculine and feminine, wisdom and love enable us to move forward in truth.

In a powerful prophecy from 1944, Deunov wrote:

The earth, the solar system, the universe, all are being put in a new direction under the impulsion of Love. Most of you still consider Love as an insignificant force, but in reality, it is the greatest of all forces! Money and power continue to be venerated as if the course of your life depended upon it. In the future, all will be subjugated to Love and all will serve it. But it is through suffering and difficulties that the consciousness of man will be awakened.

The first paradigm represents business as usual as articulated by the wealthy and powerful and is implicitly based on distorted patriarchal values prioritizing money, materialism, consumerism, exploitation, manipulation, control, dominance, violence, and an economy driven by war. The second is the rising culture representing a Great Upshift rather than the Great Reset. The first transhumanist view considers humans as carbon-based biochemical machines to be upgraded and merged with silicon machines (the Fourth Industrial Revolution), while the second recognizes the transcendent essence of the human being with a capacity for self-realization, enlightenment, and compassionate action. The first aims at what Lewis Mumford called mechanical uniformity, while the second is an expression of unity in diversity as a fundamental principle of nature.

In Deunov's view, there are four degrees of human culture (similar ideas have since been developed in spiral dynamics as well as by Ken Wilber):

- Violence: rule of the strongest—ultimately self-destructive
- Law: imposed by force, threats and fear
- Justice: excludes all privilege and preference
- Love: as the goal of the universe, equity

We see all four degrees operating in the world today, but the direction of evolution is toward love as a compass direction. The basis of equity is that "all beings form a whole as branches and leaves of the great cosmic tree of the cosmic organism." The highest levels of love he called "a Force in the Mind" where people of integrity and moral courage embody love in action, and Love as "a Principle in the Spirit" that resolves polarities and contradictions. It is this degree of Love that has the capacity to limit fear and evil. As Gandhi also observed, "Love is basically not an emotional but an ontological power, the essence of life, the dynamic union of the separated."

The four degrees of human culture correspond broadly to his outlook on the evolution of consciousness:

> Indigenous Collective Consciousness (what Owen Barfield calls original participation)
> Individual Consciousness as personality
> Collective Consciousness as solidarity
> Cosmic Consciousness as mutuality, mutual aid

Divine Consciousness as seamless spirit—what Deunov calls *unity known and felt*—and which entails the ethic of the Golden Rule: love others as you yourself would like to be loved as we are each other.

Already more than one hundred years ago, Deunov was calling for the upliftment of women:

What should be the aim of our contemporary society and our contemporary states? Women have to be raised up to the status they used to occupy in the past! Put the woman on that level where she originally was and you will see that in 125 years the world will improve. The salvation of the world is in the uplifting of the woman. The salvation of our contemporary humanity lies in the elevation of the heart.

He added that the contemporary culture was that of the mind, but the future culture will be a culture of love, of the heart. He insisted that "there is only one power in the world that is able to annihilate war and to bring in peace. What is that power? - *The woman*" (italics added). What a powerful message for our times!

Christians throughout the world have prayed for two thousand years for the coming of the Kingdom of God, which is a Kingdom of Love, a Kingdom of Wisdom, a Kingdom of Truth, a Kingdom of Freedom, and a Kingdom of Peace. This is the task and aspiration of real Christians. As Yeshua himself stated, the Kingdom is within us, the Christ Consciousness within, so we have to begin with ourselves and our immediate circle of influence. It is our individual and collective thoughts and feelings that are manifest in outer conditions.

Deunov insisted that only Love has the power to set the world to rights and that we are entering a period of liquidation where we are being subjected to the forces of extreme outer pressures and inner tensions to encourage us to discard the old and retain only good and sound elements. In order to improve conditions on earth, people must learn to love each other as brothers and sisters; only then can we live in peace and love, in brotherhood and freedom. Deep in our souls, we live in a state of expectation that the new, the transformative is on the way, what he called a Cosmic Spring.

First of all, Deunov said, you have to love the Lord with your whole heart, soul, mind, and power; then you should love your neighbor as yourself; and third, you should love your enemies. All this is already set out in the Sermon on the Mount, as Tolstoy noted. All actions carried out with love, wisdom, and light bring about harmony and concord. He reminds us that our desires and thoughts create the present world and that if we begin to talk about love and freedom, love and freedom will come, and a new story, a new narrative will be co-created and reflected through beauty and spiritual inspiration in the arts, as was the case with Deunov's own musical compositions. He said that all great musicians, poets, artists, and scientists are working for the salvation of humanity as a whole.

Would the cells and organs of the human organism function normally if they were to become isolated and individualized, breaking away from the organism? In the same way, separate individuals, societies, and nations must become conscious of themselves as a great whole, as parts of the human organism; in this way they will bring about a fundamental change in the forms of life.

Every part must realize that its success and welfare depend upon the success and welfare of the whole organism. This is the new understanding of life. This is the sun which is presently rising in human consciousness. This is the new life stream which has begun to operate and whose influence is becoming more powerful by the day in all spheres of life. It will flood all societies and nations, laying the foundation of a beautiful, noetic and harmonious life on earth.

Deunov observed that "humanity is moving towards collaboration, mutual aid, and union." He went on to raise the crucial question: "knowing how to harmonize liberty and the collective, liberty and solidarity. At first sight these seem to be mutually exclusive—their harmonic coming together is the higher idea of humanity that can only be attained through Life for the Whole." In his understanding, Love is life for the whole in a living sense, not for an abstract collective. His whole philosophy of nature is underpinned by intelligence and creativity, enacted in such rituals as witnessing the sunrise (which corresponds to an inner process of rising consciousness) and dancing the paneurhythmy, bringing mind, heart, and will into harmony through rhythmical gestures and movements. Paneurhythmy is underpinned by seven universal principles: intelligence, correspondence, vibration or movement, rhythm, cause and effect, and finally unity or relatedness.

Deunov explains that all the new ideas that are to be part of a new culture and all the vital principles that have the power to raise humanity to the level of this new life are contained in the exercises accompanied by the corresponding music. The forces of the rising culture are detailed as indestructible goodness, justice, higher noetic reason and wisdom, harmony ("all beings represent a great cosmic orchestra"), fraternity, freedom, and Cosmic Love. We will be implanted with the graft of Love, "and this world, grafted from within, will acquire a new light and a new impulse towards all other aspirations: from involution to evolution; from unending wars towards eternal peace; from hatred towards Divine Love; from egotism towards self-sacrifice." He adds that "the supreme goal of human life is that people should be free and to serve Love, Wisdom and Truth."

Human beings are a part of the whole and should live in the whole and for the whole—the basis of this is an inner union with all beings. Since his time, many sciences have been converging on the same dynamic and systemic ideas of unity in interconnected diversity whereby, as he put it, "Life is one, Mind is one, Love is one - the Universe is Unity in diversity arising from the One. The whole lives for us and we must live for the whole."

The New Culture can arrive in two ways:

> Awakening of human consciousness; inner transformation, responding to a new wave
> A path of suffering through a catastrophic breakdown

There are many people, groups, and partnerships across the planet activating an awakening of human consciousness through inner transformation, but existing dominant systems are pushing a different agenda of further mechanization and control of the human being rather than true fulfilment through spiritual realization and service to the community, in other words life for the whole. Moreover, trust can only be reestablished through truth and transparency, not through censorship and the crushing of dissent. As Ervin Laszlo has highlighted: "Living up to our sacred quest is within our grasp. The universe is one, and life in the universe is one and we are part of it. We are cosmic beings endowed with articulate consciousness. We can apprehend our quest, and we can respond to it. We can awaken to the urgent need to adopt the drive toward wholeness through coherence as our own sacred quest."

Individually, it is our quest to manifest those divine principles and qualities within by engaging our minds, hearts, and wills at the highest level. Deunov proposed that there are three kinds of life:

>Life for oneself
>Life for society
>Life for the Sublime Principle
>These correspond to:
>The law of the part—of one's own self
>The law of the majority—of the neighbor
>The law of the Whole—of God

The sacred path is serving the divine and the coming of the Kingdom of Heaven, and when we begin to live for the whole, we do everything as if for ourselves—since we are each expressions of One Life, One Mind, One Love: The appearance of Christ on earth is nothing other than the manifestation of Divine Love within our hearts and minds.

PART 2

THE SACRED ACTIONS

CHAPTER EIGHT
ACTIVATING OUR SACRED QUEST

ADAM C. HALL

In an age where existential crises loom large, posing questions about humanity's survival and its future, there emerges a profound and urgent call for action that leads to transformation, both for the individual and the whole.

"Activating Our Sacred Quest" is not simply a chapter in a book, it's an all-inclusive clarion call to awaken and evolve. We begin with a pivotal inquiry: Can humanity survive its current existential crisis? The answer is a resounding yes, but achieving that goal demands a radical shift from humanity's current state of being.

This chapter invites us on a journey of deep introspection, challenging all of us to move beyond mere survival instincts toward a path of authentic, kind, and loving engagement. Here, we'll explore the transformative power of action—not just any action, but one that aligns with the rhythms of nature and the intelligent evolution of our species. Through personal transformation and collective revolution, we will delve into the art of turning reactivity into creativity, and transforming individual, singular purpose into a unified sacred quest.

Humanity *can* and *will* survive the challenges we face. However, the humanity that will survive will not be the human collective we now know. Instead, it will be a humanity that is authentic, kind, loving, and engaged. It will synchronize and harmonize with the cycles of evolution just as Mother Earth consistently does with her seasons. We as humanity can go beyond survival to thriving, but to achieve this will require great intelligence as well as a willingness to lovingly engage with the Great Intelligence that is here to support us under every circumstance.

To thrive intelligently we must act rather than react. And we must act together rather than alone. Seems simple enough, yet as evidenced by the current state of chaos and conflict (and threat of more to come), both individual and collective action will be required. Without acting in an unseen but real relationship of unison, I believe there will be unintended outcomes of extinction proportions. Take a good hard look within and without, and I think you'll agree that as a species we have yet been unable to adopt conscientious behaviors that would prevent us from justifying our "rightness" and reacting to circumstances. For the most part, historically and currently, we have not consciously acted to evolve and resolve our challenges.

This is not a blame game. We have been hardwired for survival, reinforcing behaviors that support degeneration and death. No matter what we face, there is action to take. But we cannot take the action needed if we remain stuck in reaction. Let's begin our journey into conscious action by accepting the premise that we can first accept responsibility and then act consciously to create a flourishing planet that regenerates itself and supports us to thrive. Embracing our sacred quest necessitates that we act wisely.

What two actions can we take to transform reactive behaviors into co-creative action? And what type of intelligence will be required for us to thrive during these times of great earth changes and fulfill our individual and collective sacred quest?

The first action requires a *personal transformation.* This necessitates Transformational Intelligence. The second action demands a *collective revolution.* This requires Genius Intelligence. The former preempts all other actions that may be considered. However, without utilizing both, we will leave the future to fate. With both intelligences at play, we can lift our hands together and reach for destiny, ultimately fulfilling our sacred quest. Each of us plays a vital role. Let's remember the adage, "As the earth goes, so do I. As I go, so does the earth." Accepting our individual role comes with a sacred responsibility to tend to the earth within ourselves.

When we cross pollinate our individual and collective will, humanity's sacred quest will be launched.

Action I: Upshifting to the Sacred Quest

Externally, we physically stand on the earth. Spiritually, we stand within ourselves. When we experience earthquake tremors both on the inside and outside, our world can seem to fall apart. In order to meet the challenges of our time, we must stabilize our inner ground. To do this, we first need to unlearn those behaviors that keep us prisoners in a state of reactivity.

What must we do to stabilize the ground within in order to take intelligent action?

We must upshift away from unconscious and oftentimes dangerous reactive behaviors, thus becoming a safe, trustworthy person and reliable, planetary partner. Let's explore how you can become this evolutionary partner for yourself and others.

On my journeys, both externally and internally, I've assessed that there are two great events in life, three great questions, and one key action that we must take to become safe and trustworthy human beings. The first great event is being born. The second is discovering why we're here and then taking action. Many of us are still in search of the why. By seeking and finding the answers to the three great questions and taking the one key action, you will discover your why and your quest will be revealed. The one key action can begin right now by taking the first step and exploring the three questions for yourself. Let's begin.

The First Great Question: *How can you discover True Purpose?*
From the future's past to the present moment

In *Divine Genius: The Unlearning Curve*, I dedicated a full chapter to exploring the concept that the purpose of life is to *have* a purpose. Having purpose gives us meaning, and that meaning nurtures self-acceptance. More often than not, we seek purpose in the outer world. "I must be this" or "I must do that." We are bombarded with coercive ads and cultural and family imprints. We endlessly seek personal purpose, never finding what we seek.

The real key to understanding purpose begins with seeing that the purpose of everything and everyone in the outer world is to help point you inward. Yes, inward.

This great reward of finding your purpose can only be discovered within. Understanding the natural purpose of the outer world reveals a great secret about what true purpose really is. Since everything in the outer world points us toward our inner spiritual Self, we can conclude that this is the sole purpose of life. I found in my own relationships how true this understanding of purpose unfolds.

I married my junior high and high school sweetheart, and we have three amazing daughters. Our marriage had an important purpose. To raise a family and share our love with our children to help them grow to be flourishing people. I found a purpose as a father, husband, protector, and provider. During the course of our marital breakdown, I came to realize that my wife and children were also mirrors of what was lacking in my own family and childhood. Deep down I was lonely for connection. I felt abandoned by my parents. I feared the external world would do the same. Eventually the fear had its way and sadly the family unit broke up. When I realized that the purpose of my family was more than just a role to play, I discovered my true inner purpose: to heal and transform the pain and suffering I had felt.

Furthermore, we believe purpose can be found in what we are doing. It's important to realize that "doing life" comes as a reaction to past conditioning and beliefs (many false) about who and what we are supposed to do in order to find acceptance. Living in the future based on past events perpetuates the fatiguing cycle of endless seeking and sabotages our ability to accept our own sacred quest and take intelligent actions. So, what must you do to end this cycle?

The old idea of purpose idealizes the fear of tomorrow. We become entangled in self-made webs of pain and suffering, all the while seeking a miracle to free ourselves. But we needn't stay in this prison forever. An evolutionary miracle occurs when we awaken to our true purpose. Miracles not only are miraculous interventions but also occur with a simple shift in perception. One day we seek purpose in the outer world and the next day we discover our inner selves. When this occurs, as you may well have experienced, we awaken to a whole new way of seeing, doing, and being. Our actions henceforth show us the way to safety, trustworthiness, and reliability. This process helps us to develop our Transformational Intelligence. Almost miraculously, we become trusting of ourselves and others. We begin living in the now, discovering our purpose, and preparing ourselves to receive our own sacred quest.

We are here not only to survive the future's past but also to thrive in the present future.

When it comes to what happened yesterday or what will come of tomorrow, your true soul's purpose does not matter. Its relevance and power only matter today. In the now moment you are always free to react to the past or future, or you can act consciously without the conditioning of the past or fear of the future. Here's some good news. Because you are reading this essay and exploring your purpose and sacred quest, you have been selected by the universe to serve and act upon your soul's purpose. It has been given with ease and love.

Everything you need to fulfill your own quest is already within you. Nothing more is needed, and nothing more will be given. We seekers of the world seek to serve. And to give ourselves over fully and unconditionally to service. When the time comes that we naturally and habitually serve that which is greater than ourselves, the perpetual cycle of seeking ends. Our acts of service elegantly become the love we share with others. That love being the language of the soul. By ending your seeking and applying your will in service to your soulful true purpose, you effortlessly serve humanity.

There are as many sacred quests as there are humans.
Yet there is only One Sacred Quest that satisfies the collective soul. Love.

The Second Question, Aspect One: *How can a Sacred Quest find you?*
From doing to being

That's right. Your quest will find you, rather than the other way around. You need be only your soulful self. This part of the journey begins with self-acceptance. You are not alone. Every human being seeks acceptance, just as we all seek purpose. And as we discussed earlier in the chapter, when we find true purpose by looking within, we may end the seeking forever. We've been unaware of this truth until now, but what we've been seeking all along is to end the search for purpose. And here's the surprise you didn't even realize you were waiting for. Once you have ended the seeking for purpose, your quest can now find you. Embracing this knowing as a critical part of your journey takes courage, faith, and trust.

But fear not! You will not be lost at sea like a ship without a rudder. Remember, no longer do you need to spend your days trying to find a quest. It has already found you! A sacred quest begins with having an overall sense of direction. And have you noticed? Seeking has no direction whatsoever. Seeking searches aimlessly. *Your purpose in life is to simply end the seeking and accept yourself as you are, where you are.* Self-acceptance aligns the body, heart, mind, and spirit to receive a unique sacred quest that has been specifically coded in the soul's journey. That coding is unseen by you and based on life events in your past and present lives.

Make no mistake. When the process of seeking a purpose comes to an end, there will be an emptiness. But your specific sacred quest fills the void. Ponder this. During the seeking and acceptance process, did you ever come across a particularly profound person, place, or event that occurred during the early years in life? Perhaps you experienced the death of a parent or sibling at an early age. Maybe you felt rejected and unloved. I felt abandoned. Whatever the case may be for you, be aware that we all seek to accept ourselves and desire to break the beliefs that keep us stuck in the stories from the past. How can we break the seeking pattern for good?

By being in relationship with discomfort, our transformational intelligent nature can heal our past and clear the way for the sacred quest.

Sometimes we think that doing life and being life are two separate and distinct things. But in reality, they are the same. When we seemingly separate ourselves from being our soulful self, we reactively do things according to the past, repeating the same old patterns and believing the same old beliefs. We can disrupt those patterns by paying attention to our behaviors and reactions. If you have the interest, you can do a deep dive into the human neurological wiring system in the brain and learn how to rewire your system to change those patterns. For now, though, we are focused on the deep psychological wiring and the power you have now to upshift your state of being away from those unconscious and reactive behaviors.

Relax. You can stop efforting now. The quest you have been looking for has or will soon find you, because it has already been given. The fact that you're here now reading these words is proof of your willingness to receive. The next step in the Transformational Intelligence process occurs when the doing part ends and the being begins. (Remember, in actuality being and doing are one and the same.)

The famous book *A Course in Miracles* tells us you need not do anything. Of course, that does not mean doing nothing. It means being your soulful self. When you achieve this with grace and ease, there is nothing else to do in order to find your true purpose. In and of itself, this final step will not immediately end the *pattern* of seeking. It will, however, elevate your consciousness to the extent that the power to end the pattern will be available to you. This requires daily practice. One simple thing I strive to do, although not always successfully, is to take note when I am interacting with others. For example, when I am ordering food or at the market, do I treat others as order takers or am I meeting them, seeing them with the eyes and heart of gratitude? Every day I realize that I need to practice. The old doing self wants its way.

We've said that now the seeking has ended, the quest will be revealed. So where is it? Why can't you see it? The best clues are found in our emotions and feelings.

What moves you to passion? What stirs your action? What brings you to tears of joy? What says yes to "This is mine to do?" Being can be best understood as an awareness of body, mind, and emotions. Transformational Intelligence brings you to a state of acting from true purpose. The highest state of being any human can achieve is being on purpose in your soulful Self taking action (doing) to fulfill your own sacred quest.

Sacred Quest seekers search in unknown spaces. When we join with others in the quest, we are found by the love which guides us to destiny dawn.

The Second Question, Aspect Two:
From Reaction to Action
Being and doing are the same

From the moment of our birth, we've been trained to think that doing will get us to the end goal. In our case, the being state is the end goal. Doing and being are not the means and the end respectively. They are one and the same. The greatest trick the seeking ego plays upon us takes place when it attempts to separate the means and the end. This guarantees endless seeking because it effectively hides the being from the doing. In other words, it hides the true inner purpose by making you believe that your purpose can be found only in the outer world, in the cycle of setting and achieving goals. To end the repetitive pattern of separation of means and end, commit to upshifting this knowledge into active doing.

You can do "reactive doing," or you can do "active doing." The latter comes from the soul and the former from the ego. The reactive doer always speaks first, speaks loudest, and always reacts impulsively. The process to overcome this pattern requires us to pause, take a breath followed by another breath, and finally take a slow, doing action. Remind yourself of the Navy Seal adage, "Slow is smooth, and smooth is fast." This beautifully defines active doing. Reactive doing is fast, bumpy, and sluggish. Tune in to your physical state and your emotions. You'll easily be able to feel the difference.

Let's take this a step further to not only doing what we must do, but also being what we must be. The third and last question addresses the collective power we share when we serve our quest to help others, going far beyond the needs of the reactive, doing self. This guarantees the success of our sacred quest and the expansion of your soulful purpose. Remember, success is not an outcome. It is a process. Again, think in terms of the means and end being one and the same. So, too, the quest and the success of the quest are one and the same.

Spiritual osmosis distills that which no longer serves our evolution, rebalancing our lives with the soul's intent. Inevitably this will thrust us into our own sacred quest.

The Third Question:
What Intelligent Action shall I take?
From I to We to Us.

You need do nothing. Do you find this concept easy to accept? Perhaps not. Let's expand on this action-oriented wisdom that poses a great paradox. The "I" mentality as in me, myself, and I, reacts exclusively from the subjective lens of perception. This lens relates to our ego and personality. It is the "need-do-everything" mindset. It must control, divide, manipulate, and conquer at any cost. It asks, "What intelligent action shall I take for myself?"

The first and second great questions of this chapter are directly related to the I. The third question takes us to the "we" and "us," as well as to the objective lens of perception (rather than the subjective as in the I mentality). This objective lens of perception relates to our spirit and soul. It need do nothing in order to accomplish the being state. It simply is.

When we discover our purpose and become grounded in our authentic being, we ask ourselves, "Whom and what can I serve?" The separate I mindset transcends the beliefs of the ego and adopts the we. We then feel a part of, being one with, and becoming one with a universal community of like-minded souls. Notwithstanding this remarkable feat of personal transformation, we continue to be ensnared in the I mindset! We toggle back and forth. It's a habitual inclination. One moment we are reactive and in the next, active. Remember, active means taking action from a place of your authentic, on-purpose higher being.

Life can remain a struggle even as the sunsets of trauma and unconstructive beliefs begin to fall away. In time, shorter for some and longer for others, we begin to see the sun rising as never before. We are filled with awe and supreme appreciation. Connection, joy, peace, and newfound purpose emerge. We begin living in the present moment, finally freed from the future's past. We embrace the possibility of co-creating a destiny that once was a mere fantasy. How can we once and for all receive the long-sought-after prize of realizing our own sacred quest?

We have nothing to worry about. Conscious Evolution ultimately results in an evolutionary miracle. However, when *we* upshift, attending to and executing on our own sacred quest, we leap into an entirely new vibrational field. (You can explore more on this field in the section below titled "The Quantum Dynamics: Upshifting the Field.")

What action can you do now to experience the miracle for yourself?

Full and complete acceptance of yourself and the world as is, where is, sets the stage for a miracle. You belong. You are needed. You are seen. You are appreciated. You are unique yet not special in the us mindset. You are bigger, smarter, loved, and held in the us community of souls. The we makes up the us. When we accept and embrace this deep truth of belonging, we can find the joy of living fully in a happy and joyful state of being.

Happiness comes from our personality's desire to feel good, whereas joy comes from our soul's intent to be in service and to be intimate with others who are also aligned with their sacred quest. Happiness tends to be reactive in nature, whereas joy tends to be active. We are now entering an unprecedented period of upshifting from just happiness to joy. They are not mutually exclusive. We get to experience, feel, live, and take action on both doing happiness and being joy. How can we collectively experience happiness and joy together? By becoming and being a person of joy who shares a sacred quest.

Action II: Igniting a Collective Revolution

The Evolutionary Continuum that transforms us from separation and individual reaction to oneness and collective action has a nexus. It links all time and space into a holotropic loop. Imagine an upward spiraling circle looping around a central pillar. This image of ancient technology has been core to Indigenous culture for many millennia. The root Maya Cultures, *Maya Kara*, that once existed throughout the planet, spoke of this as the *Zuvuya*, the return path home, where all things and people return onto themselves, a return path to the stars, a scared meeting place. In the holotropic loop, those of us who are upshifting around our own sacred quest are drawn into a field where we synchronize around the central pillar or collective quest. Like breathing in and out, we create a circular flow of breath staying connected to the central pillar, yet simultaneously independent to act upon our own wants and needs.

Aquarian quantum physicists view the pillar as a nonlocalized meeting place. They call it a "spooky phenomenon." In our case, this occurs when two or more people in different places, without any known connection or knowledge of each other, begin to communicate in resonant frequencies and vibrations. The Maya called this the Language of Light. The conditions for creating such a meeting place, a "sacred field" of this sort, necessitates that a sufficient number of "pioneering souls" with sacred quests enter the upshift process like the one shared in Action I. The central pillar attracts those of like heart, mind, soul, and vibrational frequency. We are now gathering in new and dynamic ways around this sacred meeting place to coalesce around a collective quest. This place transcends gender, age, and generations.

Merging the Generational Fields

Humanity will soon reach the threshold where two or more generational fields gather around the collective quest. The Boomer and Gen X generations began this process some sixty years ago in the late fifties and early sixties. They ignited several movements all with one common quest—to free all aspects of body, heart, mind, and spirit from the oppression of existing societal boundaries. Their children, the Millennials, came into the world starting in the eighties seeded with and supported by technology that may make them the greatest generation of evolutionary minds since the Renaissance. They are birthing the fifth industrial revolution that includes the internet, artificial intelligence, and quantum computing. They are harnessing the sun and reinventing and redesigning nearly everything under it. They are the new model of humanity and new human. With these three generations coming together, a revolution now unfolds to save the planet and humanity from an evolutionary disaster.

Breaking the boundaries of past models of doing and being has become the clarion call of our time. This foreshadows the emergence of a new sacred quest.

We are no longer asking what we can do for our country and planet. We are being asked what we must do for our humanity. The world's savior will not come in the form of a person but will rise from those among us who have chosen to join together as one.

The Collective Awakening: A Regenerative Process, Not a Degenerative Result

While we are experiencing—due in large part to the Millennials—a collective awakening, we are also experiencing a collective uptick in those remaining asleep. Technology happens to be a double-edged sword allowing the old model to maintain the status quo. This can be called the degenerative evolutionary force. How can we evolve in and through the old paradigm and still maintain a world in which we survive, thrive, and fulfill our own sacred quest? How can we be the regenerative evolutionary force?

True power comes from your spiritual character. We can train our cognitive skills to excel but only our character can rise above machines and technology.

As you have likely experienced in your own awakening, the process of consciousness evolution happens in a higher vibrational field than that of unconsciousness. We are pulled forward out of the unconscious state into our awakening natural state. Consciousness can be likened to the connective tissue in the body. It holds our physical field in place while connecting each of the parts to the entire field. The Transformational Intelligence process supports those who are awakening to shed all that no longer serves their evolution and that of the emerging collective body of pioneering souls. The process makes room for a rebirth, an upshift of the species. We call this regenerative evolution.

In the evolutionary continuum, Transformational Intelligence points us toward Genius Intelligence. Every genius that has ever lived shares that they are not geniuses, but rather they are merely tapped into the Genius of the universe. Since we are part of the universe, we also have the ability to tap into its Genius. What are the secrets? How can we use this intelligence to ignite the collective awakening into a collective sacred quest?

A **successful sacred quest** is not an outcome. It is a process.

The success of our own sacred quest(s) begins and ends with a collective agreement. We move from the subjective I to the objective we to the transcendent perception of oneness. This lens of perception experiences both the *sub-* and *ob-jective*, as well as the unified field of the whole, absent of the parts. We call this the "Us Field." It creates a meeting place for our own sacred quest, and our pursuit ends where, paradoxically, it began: in oneness.

Action III: How the New Science Makes Our Quest Possible

The quantum physics theories mirror some of the core teachings of ancient spiritual systems. Specifically, the inner connectivity of all things. It helps us understand the reality of ourselves and the reality of oneness itself. This isn't possible with classical physics that deals with the everyday reality governed by Newtonian laws of motion, gravity, and so on. The science of materialism and separation makes the quest impossible. Whereas quantum physics gives us a deep understanding of oneness. There are four basic principles of quantum physics that all quanta follow. These tenets, phenomena of quantum physics, make our pursuit and activation of our collective sacred quest possible.

The Quantum Dynamics: Upshifting the Field
Creating a Unified Sacred Quest

We begin with the first tenet, *Duality*. Let's return to the visualization of a core pillar moving in and through spacetime in concert with the evolutionary spiral. This creates an upward wave that upshifts our entire human nature: body, heart, mind, and spirit. Quantum physics professes wave-particle duality. It means that all particles can behave like waves, and all waves can behave like particles. Sometimes things behave like waves, and sometimes they behave like particles. For example, what was once considered a particle, such as an electron, can sometimes also behave as a wave.

One cannot experience both the particle and the wave aspects of a quantum object at the same time. But that does not mean one cannot feel or sense both. Despite the impression of duality, there is an underlying oneness. How so?

Oneness: a felt sense of connectivity to a transcendent field of singularity.

This theory suggests that no basic distinction between a particle and a wave exists. We can also apply this understanding to our individual purpose and sacred quest (particle) and the collective sacred quest (wave). As we synchronize with the wave, we upshift into the sacred field of oneness. Earlier we explored that innate within the meeting place of oneness, we become conscious of our shared agreement on why we are here and what we are to do together.

As we gather like particles, we become subject to *Entanglement*, the second tenet. According to quantum physics, an entangled system of more than one particle is where the individual particles behave as an inseparable whole, even if they are very far apart. Imagine a battery when the positive and negative polarities are entangled to create an electrical current. We, too, are electric in nature. Quantum physics offers clues about how the illusion of separateness can be entangled with oneness.

Entanglement also occurs between people and helps explain how strange phenomena such as healing take place. People get entangled with each other when they fall in love. Just as the information present in one particle can be shared, exchanged, and mirrored with another particle, the same effect is evident in bonded people in terms of experiencing the same emotions and thought patterns. Together, we upshift the field and experience oneness as a felt sense of unity, belonging, and quest.

The Dimension of Action:
Uplifting *Us* Beyond the *I* and the *We*

Imagine a square with the dimensions of 4 x 4. The dimensions are certain and stable. In the center of the square there lies a circle. While the square remains stable, the circle acts as a wave moving in and out of space-time. Its dynamics and dimensions are unstable and uncertain. For the purpose of our inquiry, this third tenet, the *Uncertainty* principle, creates a condition that evolves the idea of I and we into a new, higher vibratory field. We are calling this the *Us Field*. Earlier we referred to this field as a meeting place. We suggested that in this sacred field a shared quest of oneness creates a collective agreement.

According to the principle of Uncertainty, we may be able to observe one physical property at a time. In our exploration, the I is the one property. There also happens to be a nonphysical property. This is called oneness. The unseen "us" aspect of ourselves remains hidden. If we are focused on the I and we, the us will become highly uncertain. The opposite also holds true. Why does this matter?

We can infer from this that life is inherently uncertain. Some aspects of reality are beyond our control. In other words, the Uncertainty principle makes reality less deterministic. It gives us the tool of free will to determine the future course of our shared sacred quest. We learn that we can change our life, our planet, and our very humanity. Nothing is predetermined. Because of this, our sacred quest becomes one with humanity's sacred quest. The field brings us together. We only need to stay focused on the "we" to overcome the uncertainty of the separate "me."

Oneness, us-ness, is an essential principle that governs how our sacred quest will succeed in the open and undetermined future.

We are fast approaching a new epoch in our evolution. Crossing the next threshold of separation from individualistic purpose and quest to collective purpose and quest is at hand. What last understanding must we have in order to step into the coming golden age of humanity?

The last principal quantum physics refers to is *Superposition.* Superposition is the ability of a quantum system—you, I, we, and us—to be in multiple states simultaneously. If two or more quantum states, you and I for example, are superposed or added together, the result will be a new quantum state, *we*. When we are superposed into a meeting place, *we* becomes *us*. One with a new unified quantum state.

Quantum superposition signifies the interconnectedness of all things.

This principle also suggests that life is full of possibilities. We can achieve our desired outcome when we direct our attention to it. Then anything becomes possible and nothing is impossible. We have reached this place in history for a reason. While that reason may be uniquely personal for each of us, its calling asks us to join together and activate our response to the sacred quest we face together.

CHAPTER NINE

ENLISTING FEMININE POWER IN PURSUING OUR SACRED QUEST

MIRELA SULA

Have you realized what motivates you in life? What makes you wake up in the morning with a burning desire to live your life fully and inspire others to do the same? We all want to control our circumstances, but we have to understand our reality before we try to change it. In order to control our environment and be in charge of our life we need knowledge of certain scientific principles and an open mind, for action is required. This knowledge is a huge asset, but what we do with the knowledge is even more important.

I always had this unconscious tendency to put my knowledge into practice as fast as it was learned. It helps to create power in our circumstances, and as a result we achieve more health, wealth, and prosperity. I have met thousands of people in my life who subconsciously told me that they are all looking to tap in that power inside them. Most of them don't know they have it, some of them know it should be somewhere inside, but they don't know how to tap into it, and there are some who search in the wrong place, which most of the time is connected with the external environment and given way to other people.

Somehow, we are all looking for something, which I believe is human nature: to find the purpose that we need in order to survive, thrive, and be fulfilled in life. This is very empowering for us. It can be the power of our voice, the power of our dreams, and the desire to leave a legacy before we decide to leave this planet. We are all born with that hidden power; it is given to us before we become aware of existing. That's why it always feels that in silence we are all trying to claim it back, because that power can give us the faith to dare and the courage to do. Until we acknowledge that power, accept it, honor it, and use it for good, we are not able to have ownership of it. It is given to us for that purpose, but it is not all given at the same time. It is there for us to earn it. It will be given to us as a portion, and we will not be able to receive more until we do something with what we already have.

In the last fifteen years, I have been consistently co-engaged with powerful women around the world. Some of them believe in their purpose, their inner power, and they are consciously working with it. Some of them are not aware of their power, some of them don't want to use it or show it, and some of them are scared of it and somehow are hiding it. I have also met women who want to be empowered but they don't know how, and women who gave up on claiming that they could ever tap into that power. But I have never met a woman that had enough confidence in her power.

I remember when one of the most powerful women that I could meet, told me, "You think I am powerful? I am not. The reality is that I am not, I simply am afraid to not use it. The power that I show is not the natural me. I wish I didn't need to look so powerful as people tell me I am. The reality is that deep inside me I don't feel powerful. I feel fragile, vulnerable, and the power that I show is a mask. Sometimes I feel so tired of it, and I often think, 'What will happen when one day I wake up and I am not able to use that mask anymore?'" I saw some tears in her eyes and felt touched that she opened up with me. In fact, I always saw her as powerful, and she has been a role model for me many times, and I believe that her power was not a mask. I told her that, and the way I see her. I don't think that she was faking her power. I have been observing and following her for a long time. She was so natural, and when she was in her zone, she was like a driven force to make people believe in her quest.

Her story has made me think a lot—when women, men, and we as humans are afraid of this word "power." If we look at the definition of the word, power, it says that "power is the ability or capacity to do something or act in a particular way." But people associate power with possession, with control, authority, and influence over others, a sovereign state, a controlling group, a force of armed men, and so on. In fact, the word power comes from the Latin *potere*, which means "to be able." But things with power are much more than able—they're able to exert a lot of force. So, it has more to do with how we see and how we express it.

When women connect with their marvelous feminine energy, that means power. They can utilize it, direct it, and make it available for the solution of every human problem. Women of the new paradigm are creating a new truth, a truth that must be told to each generation.

We are standing at the beginning of a new era. The time has arrived when women have become more confident, and we are learning how to release our power. It is like a call coming from internal sources to save the external environment around us. This is preparing the world for a new social order, a new work that we dreamed of silently for a long time.

The importance of honoring our powerful energy and accepting our power has been rather slow in reaching general consciousness, but it has arrived and already we can see it manifested in many ways, where women demonstrate their abilities to lead and create a positive impact in the world.

For a long time, women have been limited in their given zone, fulfilling their roles as wives and mothers, and the duty to follow the rules that were inherited for them. In fact, all of these are very important roles and women have played a key factor in creating a huge impact, even beyond their zone. As women, we learned how to understand the problems while running a home, and this is where all it starts, because everything derives from there, in the house, deeply inside.

The more we learned how to understand these problems, the more we grew and realized that we can contribute to the solutions as well, not only in the house but far beyond. As Margaret Thatcher, the first woman prime minister of the UK, once said, "Any woman who understands the problems of running a home will be nearer to understanding the problems of running a country." This is exactly what has happened in recent decades, when women started to break their closed circle and coming to a higher level of awareness. As a result they took more responsibilities for bringing their gifts in the service of a bigger purpose.

Everyday Battles: Every Day Is a Fresh Opportunity to Get Up and Do It Better than the Day Before

There are two types of power that we need to identify before moving further to increasing our own. There is a temporary power that helps win your everyday battles, whatever they are in your life, here and now. And there is the deeper, more lasting and altogether stronger power, which is what will help you win at life in the long run. It sometimes requires that you intentionally choose to lose this current battle so you can win the war and gain your purpose in life. The whole world is on the eve of a new consciousness, a new light, a new force. This is the new power, and more and more people are trying to learn how to tap into the cosmic intelligence so they can use their power constructively and creatively.

As we gain more understanding, we come to realize that it is there because we cannot express the power that we do not possess. This kind of power gives us a deeper meaning than before. In order to create power and influence in our reality, we need to be good observers. Through observing, we become experts of what we see, and we enlarge our mind through increasing attention and concentration.

As we take ourselves on the journey of self-discovery and self-development, we realize how much power we have inside us. So we do not need to seek power but instead claim the power that we have within. On this journey I have met so many women gaining self-confidence, which derives from creative intelligence and the courage to believe in a higher force given by nature, to create our own reality where this confidence can grow and we can think bigger.

On my journey of self-growth and finding my purpose, I have met women from all over the world who have achieved the impossible. I have met women and men who have accomplished life-long dreams, who have changed everything, including themselves.

Finding a purpose brings more hope and faith to many people who need evidence of things that before had been invisible.

In fact, life is full of many good surprises, and the good news is that we can do things to make them happen. There are two stages. First, the idea that comes into our mind as a vision, and then turning it into a reality. Six years ago, I had a big vision, that goes beyond me, and beyond a village woman from a small country full of challenges. I am glad that I dared to feed and nourish that vision and turn it into a big faith that gave me the courage to take many actions.

These are the steps that show how the power within can change everything:

> First, we need to find the human power that we already possess.
> We need to use this power to change our lives.
> Once we change our lives, we can impact the environment.
> If we manage to change and impact the place where we live, then we can master our destiny.
> Most of the time, we are victims of outer influencers or inner circumstances.

What I have noticed is that conditions are not enough to make us feel free and fulfilled; instead, it is the way we take a stand toward the conditions. And you know what, we stand where we sit, and every human being has the freedom to change at any instant. The biggest capacity that we have as human beings is to be able to acknowledge our capacity—the potential that we have inside. The capacity to create our conditions, to grow beyond them. We, as human beings, are capable of changing the world for the better, to make the best of any given situation and turn suffering into a human achievement. We are always trying to reach more, become more, do more, and have more—nothing can reach us except what is necessary for our growth. How do we attain growth?

Are we ready to let go of what is going? In order to let come what is coming, we need to exchange the old for the new, the good for the better, to receive only as we give—we cannot obtain if we are not able to master what we have.

Understanding the Feminine Essence

As we embark on this exploration, we recognize that the feminine essence holds transformative power, acting as a catalyst for the evolution of consciousness that our own sacred quest demands.

To truly grasp the significance of the feminine contribution, we must first unravel the multifaceted nature of the feminine. It extends beyond a gendered construct, enveloping a spectrum of qualities essential for navigating real human existence. Embracing the feminine encompasses valuing qualities such as empathy, compassion, and intuition present within all individuals, regardless of gender.

Throughout history and across cultures, the feminine has been revered as a source of wisdom, guiding societies through times of upheaval and transformation. In acknowledging and cherishing these inherent qualities, we pave the way for a more inclusive and enlightened approach to our own sacred quest, one that harmonizes the masculine and feminine energies within and around us.

CHAPTER TEN
HEALING AS A SACRED QUEST

Mária Sági

We are dancing on the planet. We are constantly interacting with it, drawing from it the resources we need for our life. But how are we dancing? We are not dancing well. There are better ways to dance, ways that heal us and keep us in good health. Dancing the healing dance is a way to respond to the call of our sacred quest.

The healing power of our dance with the planet is a rediscovery of timeless wisdom. It is key not just to our individual well-being, but to the well-being of the human family.

We need to take into account both the good and the bad ways in which we dance on the planet. Choosing the good ways brings great benefits. Traditional cultures have known this—they knew the healing power of living in harmony with nature. This is ancient wisdom; its roots go back to the great wisdom traditions, including those of China.

During his long reign, Huang Di, known as the Yellow Emperor of China, engaged in deep discussions with his ministers Qi Bo and Lei Gong. These wise men were dedicated to healing through a better way of living and a better way of eating. Later their successors took their inspiration from Taoist cosmology but did not abandon the basic message.

The first of the known discussions began as Huang Di asked, "I have heard that in the days of old everyone lived one hundred years without showing the usual signs of aging. In our time, however, people age prematurely, living only fifty years. Is this due to a change in the environment, or is it because people have lost the correct way of living?" Qi Bo, known as the Hippocrates of the East, replied, "In the past, people practiced the Tao, the Way of Life. They understood the principle of balance, of yin and yang, as represented by the transformations of the energies of the universe. Thus, they formulated practices such as Dao-in, an exercise combining stretching, massaging, and breathing to promote energy flow, and meditation to help maintain and harmonize them with the universe. They ate a balanced diet at regular times, arose and retired at regular hours, avoided overstressing their bodies and minds, and refrained from overindulgence of all kinds. They maintained the well-being of body and mind; and it is not surprising that they often lived for more than one hundred years."

The sages were said to have lived peacefully under heaven on earth, following the rhythms of the earth and of the universe. Those who followed the Tao lived in accordance with the rhythmic patterns of the seasons: of heaven and earth, moon, sun, and stars. They maintained the yin-yang balance of their body and their environment. This balance, as the Yellow Emperor pointed out, is the key to the healthy and sound condition of all things in the universe. The state of the world, he said, is defined by the fluctuation and variation of yin and yang forces. Under normal conditions, these forces maintain balance in the world as well as in the human body.

In modern times, the dietary aspects of maintaining the health of the body through contact with nature have been spelled out by a Japanese doctor, Sagen Ishizuka. Ishizuka advanced a theory of nutrition and healing based on the traditional Asian diet, complemented by elements from modern chemistry, biology, biochemistry, and physiology. Ishizuka's theory is based on five principles:

> Food is the foundation of health and happiness.
> Sodium (Na) and potassium (K) are the primary complementary elements of food. They determine its yin-yang quality.
> Grain is the staple food of a human being.
> Food should be unprocessed, whole, and natural.
> Food should be grown locally and eaten in season.

These practices highlight an important insight regarding the nutritional effect of dancing with the planet. Health is preserved and enhanced by attention to the rhythms and balances of nature. Food produced organically in accordance with the circadian rhythms maintains a proper balance between sodium and potassium. While Western nutrition (then as now) based itself on protein and carbohydrates, Ishizuka maintained that minerals, especially sodium and potassium, are the crucial factors. The ratio between them determines the body's ability to absorb and utilize nutrients. The key insight is that the healthy functioning of the organism depends on a proper balance of sodium and potassium.

The related key factor is the adaptation of the food we consume to the seasonal rhythms and balances of nature. If food is organic but consumed without taking into account the circadian rhythm (for example, if summer fruit from a distant land is consumed in the winter), the information in the fruit is not compatible with the organism. This results in adverse changes in the body's biochemistry and the organism becomes too acidic. If food is produced with synthetic chemicals, the information in the food is harmful to the organism. Such practices are at the root of many contemporary maladies, including obesity, diabetes, vascular diseases, and other organic disorders not limited to the classical cultures of Asia. The wisdom of Bahá'u'lláh, a Persian prophet and the founder of the Bahá'i Faith, is another shining example of deep wisdom giving birth to practical advice. The major factor is the power of nature to provide guidance for healthy living and acting.

Although it is not widely known, the Abrahamic religions were also a source of health practices, first and foremost through the teaching of Jesus. More than two thousand years ago, Jesus paid serious attention to the eating habits of his followers. He said to the Essenes, "Your body is what you eat, and your spirit is what you think."

Dietary Advice from Jesus

In the Essene Gospel of Peace, we find a segment entitled "On the Miraculous Healing of the Son of Man and on

All Secret Things of Heavens and of Earth" (based on a third-century Aramaic manuscript and old Slavonic texts). Jesus offered six injunctions for our daily diet:

1. *Eat in a healthy way in harmony with the time of day.* "Eat only when the sun is highest in the heavens, and again when it is set. And you will never see disease."
   "And when you eat, never eat unto fullness." … "So give heed to how much you have eaten when your body is sated, and always eat less by a third." … "Shun all that is too hot and too cold." … "Chew well your food with your teeth, so it become water." … "And eat slowly, as if it were a prayer you address to the Lord."
2. *Eat local foods, preferably organically produced.* "Eat not unclean foods brought from far away countries, but eat always that which your trees bear. Your God knows well what is needful for you, and where and when. And he gives to all peoples of all kingdoms for food that which is best for each."
3. *Eat foods according to the season.* "Eat always when the table of God is served before you, and eat always of that which you find upon the table of God. … God knows well what your body needs, and when it needs."
4. *Proportion also the basic foods of your meal according to the season.* "From the coming of the month of Ijar, eat barley; from the month of Sivan, eat wheat, the most perfect among all seed-bearing herbs. And let your daily bread be made of wheat, that the Lord may take care of your bodies. From Tammuz, eat the sour grape, that your body may diminish and Satan may depart from it. In the month of Elul, gather the grape that the juice may serve you as drink. In the month of Marchesvan, gath-

er the sweet grape, dried and sweetened by the angel of sun, that your bodies may increase, for the angels of the Lord dwell in them. You should eat figs rich in juice in the months of Ab and Shebat, and what remain, let the angel of sun keep them for you; eat them with the meat of almonds in all the months when the trees bear no fruits. And the herbs which come after rain, these eat in the month of Thebet, that your blood may be cleansed of all your sins."

5. *Use fresh foodstuffs as the basis of your meals.* "The foods which you eat from the abundant table of God give strength and youth to your body, and you will never see diseases. For the table of God fed Methuselah of old, and I tell you truly, if you live even as he lived, then will the God of the living give you also long life upon the Earth as was his."

6. *Sit at the table of God when you feel in yourselves the call of his angels.* "The body of the Son of Man is turned into a temple, and his inwards into an altar, if he does the commandments of God. Wherefore, put naught upon the altar of the Lord when your spirit is vexed, neither think upon any one with anger in the temple of God.

And enter only into the Lord's sanctuary when you feel in yourselves the call of his angels, for all that you eat in sorrow, or in anger, or without desire, becomes a poison in your body. Place with joy your offerings upon the altar of your body, and let all evil thoughts depart from you when you receive into your body the power of God from his table. And never sit at the table of God before He calls you through the angel of appetite."

In our day, most of us neglect the quest for eating and acting in harmony with nature. We are in urgent need of establishing more coherence with the planet. We are not dancing *with* the planet; we are dancing only *on* the planet. We are dancing to a synthetic, artificial beat. We treat the planet as a passive backdrop to our life, a mere supplier of the air, water, land, and other physical and biological resources we commandeer as if they were our possessions.

Dancing as if we were above the planet is a mistake, and it exacts a heavy toll both in regard to our health and the integrity of the planet's biosphere. Nature's equilibrium is disturbed—we see this in the changes of the climate and in the growing infertility of the land. Vast tracts of land are becoming arid, turning into desert. Hitherto habitable coastal areas are flooded, and entire islands are submerged by rising sea levels. In the polar regions, melting permafrost is emitting methane and other poisonous gases into the atmosphere. We are disrupting essential links among self-maintaining ecosystems and creating one-sided dependencies.

We distanced ourselves and diverged from the ways of life and evolution in the biosphere. We entered pathways that exceed the bounds of sustainable and healthy life and development. We became corrupted in our short-sighted search for the immediate satisfaction of self-centered aspirations. We acted without adequate regard for the consequences on others, and on nature. It is time to learn to dance to nature's beat.

We behave as if we were above and not part of the natural world. We seek to control, to dance with arbitrary steps, oriented mainly to amassing wealth and power. We need to return to the dance of a healthy life. At stake are not only our individual health and well-being, but also in the longer term the very persistence of our species. We could be heading toward crises and catastrophes that place our survival on the planet in jeopardy.

Maintaining our body in good health is a priority objective of all the healing arts, even those dealing with the health of our mind. *Mens sana in corpore sano* is an age-old wisdom tenet. We need to remember it today. If our body is not healthy, we cannot readily upshift to the higher stage of thinking and consciousness we urgently need today.

Ensuring the health of the human population of the planet is a priority objective. It is the foundation of all serious attempts to embrace our sacred quest in practice.

Let us end these reflections on healing as a basic element of our sacred quest by citing one of the most remarkable strands of evidence regarding the healing effect of direct contact with nature. The evidence comes from experience with practices known as "earthing" and "grounding." These practices have been part of the culture of Indigenous peoples. Today they are rediscovered by scores of medical practitioners, including qualified doctors and natural healers.

Grounding proves to be an effective remedy for inflammatory processes and aging in general. We know that it feels good to walk barefoot in the forest or in wet sand, to bathe in a lake or the sea, to hug trees, or to pet a dog or a cat. Stress is reduced. We feel energized, ready for action. Now we know why this is so.

The earth's electric charge is negative because the planet's atomic matter is dominated by negatively charged particles. Our natural environment is filled with negatively charged electrons. As we move away from the ground, the energy of negatively charged electrons weakens. At the same time, the earth's atmosphere is positively charged, thus creating a tension between the atmosphere and the ground. We can experience the effect of this tension. When our skin comes into direct contact with the ground, we are in contact with the negative pole of the planet-wide battery. This protects us from electrostatic charge. The latter is created when we rub against plastics, such as synthetic fabrics or carpeting. Strong charging can cause our hair to burn and produce other unwelcome effects.

Experiments demonstrate that electrons assimilated from the earth are not only fast-acting antioxidants, but when in contact with the earth's electric field, they also help to synchronize the hormonal rhythms of the body.

Products made of synthetic fibers have severed us from electric sources, from contact with the earth and its stock of electrons. Earthing is a way to transfer electrons and thereby fortify mitochondria and create optimum levels of adenosine triphosphate in our body's cells. Grounding or earthing bring important benefits. It reduces cardiovascular risk and cardiac arrest.

The above examples tell us that if we wish to live a healthier life, we need to become more coherent with the world around us—more aligned with nature and the universe. We must restore our dance to the planet, dancing *with*, and not just *on*, planet earth. Doing so is a crucial element of responding to humanity's sacred quest at this critical point of our tenure on the planet.

Reference

Stephen T. Sinatra, Drew S. Sinatra, Step, and Gaetan Chevalierd: Grounding–The universal anti-inflammatory remedy. Biomed J. 2023 Feb; 46(1): 11–16. Published online 2022 Dec 15. doi: 10.1016/j.bj.2022.12.002. PMCID: PMC10105021. PMID: 36528336

CHAPTER ELEVEN
TAKING DOWN THE WALLS AROUND OUR HEART

BRADLEY NELSON

Can you think back to a time in your life when you felt like your heart was going to break? When you felt so grief-stricken or hurt that you didn't think you could stand it? Do you remember the physical sensation that you felt during that experience? You may have felt as if an elephant were sitting on your chest, or that you couldn't breathe. Unfortunately, these feelings that we often refer to as "heartache" or "heartbreak" are quite universal, as there seem to be words that describe these physical sensations in every language around the world.

When we are experiencing deep grief, hurt or loss, it can actually be an assault on the deepest part of our being, on our hearts. These feelings of heartbreak can be so uncomfortable, so foreign, and so difficult to deal with, that they often result in the formation of an energetic "wall" designed to protect the heart from these profoundly negative emotions.

New research is beginning to reveal that the human heart is much more than simply a muscular pump that circulates our blood. Indeed, it appears that the human heart is a second brain that holds the key to true inner healing, as well as reaching our highest levels of abundance.

Ancient peoples believed that the human heart was the core of our being and the seat of our soul. They believed that the heart was the source of our ability to give and receive love, as well as the repository of our deepest creative powers and intuition.

In the Bible, for example, we read, "As a man thinketh in his heart, so is he," and "the Lord sees not as man sees, for man looks on the outward appearance; but the Lord looks on the heart." The Egyptians believed that after death each person passes through a ceremony that they referred to as "The Weighing of the Heart," in which the deceased's heart is "weighed" to discover what kind of life they lived.

In the West, we have traditionally tended to dismiss these ancient beliefs as mere poetic license, as the feeble attempts of unsophisticated peoples to explain psychological processes of which they had no understanding.

However, it seems that the ancients may actually have been far more correct than we have imagined.

For example, heart transplant recipients from the very beginning have reported strange symptoms, including changes in their music, food, and entertainment preferences, as well as handwriting changes. Many have even reported receiving memories that were not their own.

There are thousands of stories of "cellular memory" like these. Is the heart more than a simple, muscular pump? The answer may lie in new developments in modern technology.

The heart is the most powerful emitter of magnetic energy in the body. In fact, the heart creates a magnetic field that extends around the body up to twelve feet in diameter, according to measurements made using magnetocardiography.

Scientists on the cutting edge of these new technologies believe that the heart can be considered to be a "second brain." They believe that the heart is sending messages to all the cells of the body continuously, and that the "brain in your head" is obeying the messages that are being sent by the "brain in your heart."

A number of years ago I received a powerful message from above that revealed to me something that I would never have imagined. My wife had accompanied me to a conference on magnetic healing, where I was one of the slated speakers. Early on the morning of the conference, she woke me and told me that she'd had a dream. In her dream were three symbols. She awakened with the understanding that these three symbols had to do with her own health and well-being. She asked me if I would help her to decipher her dream, and I agreed to do so. I was in the midst of helping her when suddenly something happened to me that was unlike anything I had ever experienced before.

I suddenly saw before me, in a waking vision, a beautiful hardwood floor. I could see this floor very clearly. It was the most beautiful floor that I've ever seen in my life. It appeared to have many coats of polish and was mirror-like in appearance. I did not imagine this! It suddenly was there before me. This vision of this gorgeous hardwood floor persisted for several minutes. The moment I first saw this floor, an understanding came into my mind that my wife's heart was somehow "beneath" this floor.

As you might imagine, I had absolutely no idea what this meant! I told my wife what I was seeing and understanding, and she had no explanation for it either. We prayed, asked God for help, and began testing her subconscious mind through muscle testing. Within about thirty minutes, we figured out what it all meant.

My wife was born into a very volatile family. Her father was always flying into a rage about something, and as a result, no one felt safe. By the time my wife was two years old, she had felt like her little heart was going to break often enough that her subconscious mind—acting entirely on its own—created a Heart-Wall, literally a "wall of energy" around her heart, for protection.

This "Heart-Wall" did its job, but there was a price to be paid. Because of this wall of energy around her heart, it was more difficult for her to give and receive love. Because of this wall around her heart, she always felt somewhat isolated. Even with friends whom she had known for many years, she never quite felt like she really belonged. In social groups she always felt like she was on the outside looking in. It was difficult for her to feel positive emotions, but easy for her to feel negative emotions. She dealt with depression and anxiety and other negative feelings that she couldn't seem to shake.

We found that her Heart-Wall was made of multiple layers of trapped emotional energy or "trapped emotions," from difficult experiences she'd had in her life. By releasing these trapped emotions one at a time, we were able to reduce the size of this wall around her heart, and finally, to eliminate it entirely. When it was gone, the changes she felt were powerful. Suddenly, she felt like she belonged for the first time in her life. It became much easier to feel positive emotions, and her depression and anxiety disappeared.

At first, I thought this phenomenon might be unique to my wife. I was so wrong! Since then, I have found that approximately 93 percent of people suffer from this phenomenon. I have personally seen profound changes occur in people's lives when their Heart-Walls are dismantled.

When trapped emotions and Heart-Walls are released, people sometimes say it's like they can finally feel again. They can give and receive love freely for the first time in a long time. In that state, very interesting and wonderful things can happen.

The most common physical symptoms that are associated with having a Heart-Wall are neck pain and stiffness, heaviness in the chest, shoulder pain, and pain in the upper back. These symptoms occur because the negative emotional energies that make up the Heart- Wall distort the normal energy field of the upper body, interfering with the circulation of blood and lymph, as well as the flow of energy in the acupuncture meridians.

I have also found that having a Heart-Wall will depress the immune system, making the body more susceptible to infection and all manner of diseases. I believe this occurs because a Heart-Wall will interfere with the heart's communication with the cells of the body, hampering their ability to function normally. If you've been diagnosed with a disease of any kind, it's very likely that a Heart-Wall is part of the constellation of underlying causes.

Is a wall around your heart contributing to physical illness or disease? Is your Heart-Wall hampering your ability to give and receive love? Is it interfering with your ability to feel good emotions, or is it contributing to your feelings of isolation? Is it creating depression, anxiety, or self-sabotage? Is your Heart-Wall interfering with your ability to succeed?

If you are at all frustrated with your love life, your social life, your health issues, or the level of financial abundance that you have been able to attain, a Heart-Wall may be a big piece of the puzzle.

The price we pay for having Heart-Walls is incalculable. How many people have led disconnected and lonely lives due to the walls around their hearts? How many people have not experienced the joy of finding love in their lives? How many have been abused?

Heart-Walls can lead to depression, divorce, and abuse. The patterns of abuse that are created can pass from generation to generation, causing all manner of pain and destructive behavior.

The result of Heart-Walls on a larger scale leads to misunderstanding, prejudice, hatred, and brutality. On a global scale, Heart-Walls lead to ethnic cleansing, nation against nation, terrorism, and war.

There is altogether too much isolation and violence, too much sorrow and pain in this world. When I walk down the street, I see so many people with tight, clenched jaws or angry, resentful expressions, acting out their pain and frustration any way they can. The news is filled every night with one story after another about people whose hearts must be barricaded behind strong walls for them to do the things they do.

Widespread depression is another common side effect of Heart-Walls and trapped emotions. In the United States of America alone, it is estimated that between thirteen and fourteen million people suffer from depression.

It is the leading cause of disability in American women. Nearly 15 percent of those women will ultimately commit suicide. Among children and young adults—between ten and twenty-four years old—suicide is the third leading cause of death. By releasing trapped emotions and removing Heart-Walls, we have seen cases of severe depression eliminated once and for all. We have seen marriages saved, abuse stopped, and lives turned around. We've seen beautiful, loving relationships begin. We've seen kids make better choices. We've seen peace restored.

Imagine how this world will change when we can open enough people's hearts to create a critical mass, perhaps only thousands of us, that will be enough to help transform this planet forever. Working toward removing the trapped-emotion-generated walls from around our heart is truly to meet our sacred quest on the planet.

There is no doubt in my mind that what I've learned about trapped emotions and Heart-Walls comes from above and that it is meant to bless many lives in these critical times. I feel blessed to have been led to discover a method that has such a powerfully transformative effect on people's lives and grateful to share and bring this information to light. Removing the walls around our heart is part of our sacred quest for humanity.

CHAPTER TWELVE
BRINGING OUR SACRED QUEST HOME

SUZANNE GIESEMANN

One of the most frequently asked questions by those who ponder the deeper meaning of life is the question we ask also in this book: What is my purpose? The question arises because there is something within each human that knows we exist for a reason. Our awareness that there is purpose in our existence is what distinguishes us from other species on the planet.

Our relatively highly developed consciousness allows us to make decisions and take actions that deliberately advance our species and support the continuation of life. Thus, by focusing on what makes us unique, we have the answer as to our purpose: To paraphrase the sacred quest outlined in the first chapter of this book, we are here to use our higher level of evolution to create something more beautiful than what has already been created.

In other words, we exist to experience life fully and to consciously further its evolution as we do so. We recognize self-awareness as a tool that we can use to achieve this lofty goal, if only we will awaken to its power.

This is the quest that Ervin Laszlo and the contributors to this book have so eloquently laid out. It is a task made sacred because we understand the preciousness of life as well as its precarious nature.

The term *sacred* implies that one regards something with reverence. Rare is the human who isn't stopped in their tracks by the majesty of a snow-capped mountain, energized and inspired by a thundering waterfall, or awed by a newborn baby's cry. We are endowed with an innate appreciation for the miracles found in nature, not the least of which is the human body. We intuitively know that we are far more than the sum of our parts.

The question then becomes: How are we doing with our sacred quest?

Some claim that we are a remarkably evolved form of life in this corner of the universe. Relative to other species on the planet, this may be true, but objective observers beyond our space-time reality might struggle to take such a claim seriously.

What highly evolved species would so disrespect the sanctity of life that its members kill each other in mass numbers over money, power, territory, or differences in beliefs? What advanced beings would mistreat their bodies by willingly ingesting toxic substances, selfishly abusing natural resources, and treating their host planet and other resident species with blatant disregard?

Clearly, there is much room for growth.

For decades, Ervin Laszlo has tirelessly shared the latest discoveries in science and spirituality to motivate us to be better stewards of the gift of life. His books reveal a multidimensional world beyond our space-time reality. He and other leading-edge thinkers show beyond any doubt that we are not the independent beings that our physical senses have deceived us into thinking we are.

Unfortunately, we humans are notoriously slow to change deeply entrenched and restrictive belief systems. Despite the efforts of evolutionary wayshowers, most humans continue to allow their physical senses to hold them prisoners to a worldview that is seriously outdated.

Plato's "Allegory of the Cave" is ideal for understanding how our limited human viewpoint keeps us trapped. The story shares the plight of a group of men imprisoned in a cave for the entirety of their lives. They are chained so that they face the back of the cavern. When objects pass by a fire behind them, they see shapes and movement on the blank wall and give names to the shadows.

Their reality consists only of the cave, the wall, the shadows, and each other. They don't realize there is something beyond their current experience projecting the shadows they see.

Plato wrote this allegory in 375 BCE, showing that philosophers have been pondering influential realms beyond our own for thousands of years. Yet, in our current era, those who question the existence of an interactive reality beyond the physical "walls" of our planet remain in the minority, often scorned and derided, despite advances in science proving the interconnectedness of all life.

We now have ample evidence to confirm that at the deepest levels of reality, nothing is separate. We know that consciousness—not physical matter—is primary and limitless, and that we are interdependent expressions of Life. The age-old axiom that "what we do to another we do to ourselves" is more than a philosophical platitude. It is now a fundamental scientific truth.

Still, it has taken the scientific community decades to acknowledge that quantum entanglement is real and that everything is connected as part of one unified whole. In 2022 the Nobel Prize in Physics was awarded jointly to Alain Aspect, John Clauser, and Anton Zeilinger for experiments completed in the 1900s.

Historically, ideas and knowledge that would bring us together have been relegated into corners as dark as the ages in which they arose. The evolution of unity consciousness requires more than just an elite core of scientists or enlightened sages who understand the concept of oneness. Information about our true nature needs to flow down to the masses.

Thankfully, people from diverse walks of life are now questioning reality and exploring the nature of life and consciousness. As a result, belief systems are changing and doing so at an accelerated rate. The internet and social media provide access to esoteric information and innovative thinking in every home, which is precisely where efforts to unite humanity in a common quest must spread.

Taking Personal Responsibility

The man of Self-realization knows a bliss
that cannot be compared to anything in this world.
It is an incomparable happiness that cannot be described in words.
—Paramahansa Yogananda

As we look around us and see the way humans continue to ignore and disrespect our divine nature, it is easy to wonder if we are making any progress at all in evolving. The answer is yes. We have advanced from the dark ages, a period of little scientific and cultural advancement, but there is unarguably room for improvement.

If we were to speak in terms of the numbers of people on earth today who are awakened to our true nature versus those who are still "asleep," we might wryly refer to our present era as the *dim* age. The light of consciousness is burning brighter than in past eras, but we are still focusing upon the shadows on the wall.

We have progressed from the "infancy" of humankind through early childhood—from egocentrism to group-centric consciousness. On average, the current developmental age of *Homo sapiens* is akin to adolescence or early adulthood.

Greater numbers of people are aware of the need to think beyond their group or tribe and see themselves as part of a global community. We will achieve "adulthood" when enough people evolve to the awareness of our shared cosmic consciousness.

We can accelerate this growth process by embracing 21st-Century Spirituality®. This requires updating our personal belief systems with the latest scientific discoveries about the nature of consciousness and the underlying reality. These findings, blended with ancient spiritual truths, bring us to a *knowing* that we are all connected at a level beyond this earthly realm.

Spirituality is not about becoming a better "me." It is about realizing that what we call "me" and "my mind" is part of a greater shared field of awareness, or the one Mind of consciousness.

Spiritual teachers often use the term "light" as a metaphor for this omnipotent, omnipresent, omniscient consciousness. To come to know that we are a spark of this divine flow of Light and cannot be separated from it is called *enlightenment.*

An awakened or enlightened person realizes that we operate in a physical body as what appears to be a separate self, but we are never separated from the ultimate Self shared by all.

This is Self-realization.

Raising the Quality of Our Consciousness

Like IQ, every human starts life with a certain QC, or quality of consciousness. What differentiates us from other species on the planet is our ability to intentionally raise our QC—to turn up our light and help it burn as brightly as possible. As we do so, we illuminate all those around us.

People with a low quality of consciousness see the world as hopeless, sad, frightening, or frustrating. They feel and act like powerless victims. They feel that their self-worth depends on their profession, title, and role. They have a low tolerance for other points of view and see disagreement as a threat. They exclude those who don't adhere to their own view and see their nation, religion, or race as more blessed than others.

More awakened humans experience life as exciting, challenging, and stimulating. They know that love is created within. The result of this awareness is true and abiding happiness.

One with a high quality of consciousness reaps what are referred to biblically as "the fruits of the spirit," which include patience, kindness, goodness, and self-control—all of which help to fulfil our quest of the evolution of our species. As each human works to raise the quality of their consciousness, everyone benefits. This is why spirituality must begin at home—in the heart of each of us.

How do we raise our quality of consciousness? By living The Awakened Way®. This approach to life is not a religion or a philosophy but a mindful path that is based on three fundamental truths:

We are not "only human."

We are part of a multidimensional web of consciousness connecting all that is.

The healing and creative Force of the universe is Love.

This Force—the aspect of us that knows life has meaning—propels us ever onward, ever upward. Just as a plant will push its way through a crack in a sidewalk, always seeking the light, we experience a natural push to discover these fundamental truths within us.

We come to the awareness of our true nature and increase our QC by consciously taking these steps:

Expanding Our Awareness

Consciousness is malleable. Awareness can be focused like a camera lens into different states. The normal mode of operation for most humans is to perceive experiences through the narrow lens of normal waking consciousness using only the physical senses.

The dream state reveals that there are alternate ways of perceiving reality. When dreaming, we are conscious of experiences, yet reality unfolds with a different operating system from what we call the physical world.

For example, in normal waking consciousness, time unfolds linearly from past to present to future. We are restricted by gravity and geography, requiring physical effort to get from point A to point B. In dreams, there is no sense of time, and we can experience what appear to be different geographical locations or environments in rapid succession.

The brain acts as a filter of consciousness, restricting awareness of the limitless, creative ways in which consciousness can unfold. Meditative practices and psychedelic drugs are two methods by which one can bypass the brain's normal filters and experience realities or dimensions with uniquely definable characteristics.

Few humans venture beyond normal waking consciousness and the dream state. Fear or ignorance of a greater reality is holding us back from discovering far greater capacities for growth that are available to all. A bit of curiosity, training in accessing alternate states of consciousness, and the willingness to step outside of restrictive belief systems reveal that we are multidimensional beings with unused capabilities.

Those who publicly share near-death experiences speak with confidence of the continuity of consciousness beyond the physical death of the body. Evidence-based mediums further validate the existence of a reality that allows one's personal storyline to continue after death, albeit in nonphysical form.

The formless, more spacious aspect of consciousness is known as the soul. The so-called astral realm allows the soul far more conscious control of its environment than when expressed through a body. With the expanded awareness afforded by experiences in the nonphysical realms, one becomes acutely aware of the connectedness of all life. This lack of separation is the very definition of love, which reveals itself as the driving Force behind all of creation.

Upshifting Our Perspective

Henry David Thoreau correctly stated that the mass of men live lives of quiet desperation. A life filled with frustration, disappointment, and misery is a direct result of identifying with the physical body and one's chosen role rather than shifting to a higher perspective and discovering the self beyond our limited stories.

With a simple change in consciousness born of a free will choice, we can shift from feeling dissatisfied and disconnected to being aware that we are part of an intelligent, creative, benevolent universe and that we are lovingly guided every moment.

Albert Einstein stated that no problem can be resolved at the level at which it originated. We can accelerate the evolution of our species by exploring higher states of awareness where insights and guidance are readily available.

As we maintain greater presence and follow the guidance that arises from within, we make choices that are in alignment with our highest self and enjoy a purpose-filled existence. We experience a sense of completeness and connection with everything and everyone around us.

Such a joy-filled, purposeful life is available to anyone as the result of living The Awakened Way. Once we regularly and intentionally shift awareness to reality beyond the confines of normal human awareness, we become the conscious creators we are born to be. We step outside the prison of the limited human mind and access the wisdom of our shared higher consciousness.

Where we focus our attention determines our reality. When we attend a symphony, we can choose to focus on one instrument, one section, or the entire orchestra. Likewise, with presence we can become aware when we are perceiving reality through a limited human lens or the more expanded lens of higher consciousness.

A simple shift to expanded perspectives provides access to greater possibilities and higher choices. These more readily result in feelings of peace, joy, and the bliss of total connection with all that is. Such experiences become the norm instead of an elusive goal when one makes the choice to live consciously.

Aligning with Our True Nature

As awakened humans, we see the world differently. We live from the awareness that we are both human and divine and that we are in a physical body to be the presence of love. This is wholeness.

We recognize that black and white exist, and that these and all opposites are part of the ongoing unfolding and enfolding of life. There is less judgment of experiences as good or bad. Instead, we see all sensations, thoughts, and feelings as part of an endless process of becoming.

Humans learn and grow through trial and error by dancing and flowing with the opposites. We make choices and experience their effects mentally, emotionally, and physically. We align with our higher nature beyond these divisions by making choices that benefit the greatest and highest good.

In the simplest terms, we base all decisions on the answer to the most fundamental question: How would love act?

When we are aligned with our true nature, the ever-present Light of awareness within cleverly reveals the answer. We experience contentment because our thoughts and actions promote growth and connection.

Alternatively, when thinking and acting in ways that do not promote growth, we experience feelings such as guilt, shame, and regret. These are not punishments. They are evolution's indicators that we are out of alignment with our true nature. Feelings are nature's built-in guidance system, directing us to make higher choices.

No Longer Identifying with Obsolete Stories

The body is a temporary costume that allows consciousness to express itself through various roles and relationships. Each of us enacts archetypal story lines with characters and scenarios that repeat themselves across lifetimes.

Challenges arise when we don't realize we are acting out roles. Like method actors, we forget that we can use expanded states of awareness to metaphorically step off the stage. Suffering is the result of getting caught up in "the story of me."

When we no longer identify with our stories, we enjoy a fully opened heart, seeing other's negativity as ignorance of our true nature. An awakened being knows the ego has a role to play and does not engage the unawakened ego of others. This comes with no feelings of superiority, but with sincere compassion. We live in the present, free of emotional addictions and attachments.

The key to freedom from victimhood and powerlessness is coming to know that we are whole and complete at our most essential level. The three E's of living The Awakened Way provide a task-oriented way to fulfill the sacred quest elaborated in this book. We *need to educate, experience, and engage* in the following ways:

Educating Ourselves about the Nature of Consciousness and the Greater Reality

It's easy to take what we call reality for granted. We willingly accept certain statements about the way the world operates based on appearances, even when we know they're not true. Does the sun really rise and fall? Is the body solid, or is it a swirling pattern of information and energy at a deeper level? Could it be both?

Part of our sacred quest as humans on earth at this time is to question our idea of reality. We are here to use our innate curiosity and grow as a result. This is an exciting time to be on earth. Scientists are no longer imprisoned for sharing revolutionary theories. Women are no longer burned at the stake for revealing the underlying reality.

The evolution of technology is propelling our species' evolution. The world is literally at our fingertips. We can now use the World Wide Web to discover and share information about the infinite web of consciousness.

Learn from the experts. Read online journals, articles, books, and blogs. Watch videos. Listen to firsthand accounts of those who have had veridical adventures in consciousness. It has been scientifically proven that hearing others' stories opens one to the possibility of having similar experiences. This leads to the second E ...

Experiencing the Greater Reality for Ourselves

It's useful to discuss theories of consciousness and benefit from learning of others' experiences. Nothing can raise our own quality of consciousness as quickly or effectively, however, as spending personal time in expanded states of awareness.

Belief, intention, and *attention* are the three keys to making the connection with Higher Consciousness. First, believe that your normal waking state of consciousness is one of limitless states that you can access. Second, set and hold the clear intention to access these higher states as needed for assistance, comfort, and healing. Third, focus and hold your attention beyond your story while exploring other realms.

As long as we are experiencing life in a body, the brain will filter out awareness of the higher dimensions. Seek out and practice methods such as meditation and mindfulness that will allow you to temporarily bypass that filter. The resulting experiences are transformational.

Once we regularly access the part of us that never changes, we more easily notice the contrast between human nature and our true nature.

Engaging with Higher Consciousness

If you make the effort to educate yourself about the greater reality and experience it for yourself, you may well come to experience other expressions of the one true Self. You will discover that everything that exists is the experiences of the one Mind of awareness seen and expressed through limitless viewpoints.

Why stop with the human point of view? We limit our growth when we allow fear of the unknown or restrictive thinking to keep us trapped in a limited paradigm. There are other lenses through which to view reality. When sentient consciousness sends us evidence of realities beyond our own, we can make the choice to investigate further or dismiss these phenomena.

We are always being guided. We are never alone, for the expressions of consciousness are limitless.

A Commitment to SIP

To bring our sacred quest home, we need to experience expanded states of consciousness as a regular part of our daily lives. Traditional religions reserve one day per week to worship the divine. Our sacred quest requires a moment-by-moment devotion to realizing that all are worthy of worship.

A simple practice called the SIP of the Divine®, where SIP is an acronym for "Sit in Peace," can demonstrate the truth of our innate divinity. Set aside three minutes each day to sit quietly and observe the nature of the mind. In so doing, one discovers that sensations, thoughts, and feelings arise and subside without our conscious control. We soon notice there is an observer within that is beyond the experiences of body and mind.

In the silence, as subjects and objects merge, we experience our innate wholeness. With the gift of this readily accessible state, we can engage in higher aspects of the Self and ask for guidance. Engaging higher consciousness with the simple question, "What do I need to know right now?" results in unexpected insights and previously obscured connections.

The many benefits of this simple practice soon become apparent. We experience more peace throughout the day. Intuition increases. Our sense of connection with others and with our own inner guidance increases. As a result, three minutes a day may become five, ten, or twenty minutes spent shutting out the outer world so as to explore more of the inner world. As we come to know that we are "This"—pure Awareness *being*—we gain access to worlds upon worlds.

It is no small thing to discover through direct experience that we are not only human.

Restoring Our Dance to the Planet

Raising our quality of consciousness takes commitment and conscious effort, but the rewards quickly reveal themselves. As we shift to living the consciously connected and divinely guided life that The Awakened Way promises, we:

see creation as the expression of one Mind;

seek the good of all beings and desire to be of service;

identify with the soul and not the body;

experience profound insights and frequent synchronicities;

have regular and direct access to higher consciousness;

view our lives from the perspective of the neutral inner witness;

enjoy an intuitive sense of connection with others;

gain information from beyond the physical senses;

are self-reliant instead of relying on the advice of others; and

lose all fear of death.

Such a life is indeed sacred. Such a life is possible for each of us, for if we can imagine such a life, we can create it for ourselves. That is how consciousness works.

Ervin Laszlo likens our earthly experience to a dance with the planet. We experience it as harmonious when we flow in balance with the eternal cycles and rhythms that flow through all that is.

Evolution is a natural process. Life bursts forth to experience its fullness. We are driven to create something better from what has come before. We see the results of this evolutionary holotropic attractor in ongoing advances in medicine, the arts, and all other creative expressions of higher consciousness.

We cannot help but evolve in this ongoing dance of LIFE—an acronym for Love in Full Expression. Rather than stepping on each other's toes as we move about our earthly dance floor, may we pause ever so slightly after each step in this ethereal waltz with awareness:

Step, pause, listen …
Step, pause, listen …

And in those brief but essential pauses, we attune to the ever-present evolutionary impetus, the wholeness-seeking guidance that leads us twirling and spiraling eternally onward and upward.

CONCLUDING REFLECTIONS AND EXPLORATIONS

More on the New Story Inspiring and Supporting Our Sacred Quest

Robert Atkinson, Shannon Winters, and Kurt Johnson from Light on Light Publications

Humanity is awakening to its sacred quest. Ervin Laszlo, in this much-needed reminder of our inherent responsibility to adopt a goal worthy of our role on this planet, points to a new story from science, fully evident in nature, that all life evolves with a goal-directedness. That innate goal built into evolutionary processes throughout the universe is to create greater and lesser systems of integral coherence, all in harmony with each other, and all in accordance with a wholeness-creating impetus in the universe.

It is in creating this new story that Charles Eisenstein proposes a new sacred quest to animate our civilization. Requiring a radical change in our thinking, it would be a story that we discover and identify as woven into reality, that we choose to align with as agents of its continued unfolding. This new story is emerging within us; it beckons us to respond.

Guiding the unfolding of this new story is of paramount importance to Suzanne Giesemann. She says our sacred task is to consciously further evolution in the direction it is already designed to go. We can get out of our own way by leaving the dark cave we have existed in for too long and step into the light of a new day. We can no longer afford to identify with obsolete stories.

These important points are exactly why we need to reclaim the tradition of unitive narratives the First Peoples lived by when their guiding stories embodied the values and principles characterizing the harmony, unity, and wholeness of creation they observed all around them.

A unitive narrative is grounded in unitive consciousness and is the basis for a holistic, unitive worldview. But as communities grew, expanded, spread out, and became more focused on differences, divisive narratives emerged that supported separation. After many millennia of conflict and chaos, as we approach a consciousness of global integration, we are in dire need of narratives that bring about unity and identity.

As the storytelling species, we think in story form, speak in story form, and find meaning and purpose through our stories. This is central to who we are to our core. When meaning, purpose, and direction are missing from our stories, personally and collectively we are lost, without a rudder to guide us. We need to expand, deepen, and reframe our identity based on the demands of our time.

A unitive narrative inspires, reflects, validates, supports, and guides the reality of the inherent unity-in-diversity of the human family and all life as we experience and come to know this in everyday life. A unitive narrative for our time will be in harmony with the evolutionary impulse, returning us to wholeness.

Expressing and representing the unified nature of reality, unitive narratives facilitate the process of transformation. Beyond the basic story pattern of beginning, middle, and end, a deeper level of story takes us through the pattern of *beginning*, *muddle*, and *resolution*. The muddles, or challenges, we face represent the core of the pattern that brings the process of transformation to its completion, or resolution.

This pattern, also found in mythology, mysticism, ritual, and psychology, centrally locates transformation within its core, connects us to the cycles of nature, and at the same time heightens our desire to "give back" and "lift up" others in whatever ways we can.

In this context, a unitive narrative keeps us on track, on the path of truth-telling and following the way of unity. It connects to all the other narrative forms we are so used to in the following ways: *myth* is a metaphorical representation of a truth to live by; *story* is a weaving together of a sequence of events that may or may not be true; *narrative* is the form, structure, or pattern a myth or story is told in; and a *unitive narrative* is a truthful personal or collective story of living into the wholeness of the unified field of existence all around us.

The stories we live by need to carry the possibilities we collectively envision as the fulfillment of our dreams. We need narratives that illustrate how diversity is in our DNA, how we have from our earliest days lived with a deep regard for the natural world, and how we belong to a planet that benefits from our stewardship. We need narratives that illustrate our unitive relationships with each other and all life.

We live for—and can't live without—narratives that explain reality as it is, as a unified whole. For our narratives to reach this deeply, to bring about unity, we need to recognize that we are one human family, sharing a common homeland.

A unitive narrative is founded on the convergence of the latest scientific breakthroughs and the earliest universal spiritual wisdom. We now understand that all things evolve toward ever greater levels of interdependence, characterized by unity-in-diversity at each expanding level. Evolution's path is a spiral, like the cycles of nature, always in the direction of wholeness.

Acknowledgment of the whole enables us to look deeper and probe fundamental truths of essential relationships throughout the universe. There we see that the physical realm we exist in cannot have created itself. The universe, at all levels of existence, arose from deeper nonphysical causes.

This understanding gives us a felt sense of unity with all life and unity with the ineffable source of all being. A unitive narrative invites us to embrace the wisdom of the complementarity and wholeness of seemingly opposing forces, such as feminine and masculine attributes, enabling us to achieve unity in the diversity of expressions on our way to a consciousness of wholeness through which we carry out our actions in the world.

A unitive narrative recognizes our fundamental interbeing, interconnectedness, and interdependence with the whole community of our planetary home, Gaia, and with the entire universe. In addition, this empowers us to envision and co-create a love-based rather than separation-based future in which regenerative and sustainable development, unitive justice, and peace are natural outcomes of a world that works for all beings and our planetary home.

Unitive narratives are needed now more than ever to lead us through a process of shifting the focus from individual well-being to collective well-being. In our time, the part no longer takes precedence over the whole. As a result, both are completely interdependent. Exclusive emphasis on any one part endangers the whole.

A unitive narrative gives us a deeper commitment to ensuring earth's well-being, as a living organism, as we understand more clearly that this depends upon collaborative relationships and dynamic co-evolutionary partnerships on a planetary scale.

Since humanity's spiritual evolution began with unitive narratives, those stories that maintained harmony and unity by keeping people aligned with the nature of reality, it is fitting that humanity's sacred quest is now framed by the new story from science, echoed throughout nature, that provides the needed framework for a unitive approach to all actions we take toward harmony, balance, and unity on the planet.

We are pleased to offer this publication that intends to further our understanding of the direction of evolution and our critical role in ensuring the realization of its intended outcome. In this and all our publications, we of Light on Light fully support this sacred quest.

TO DANCE OUR SACRED DANCE: PRACTICAL ADVICE FROM A PERSONAL TRANSFORMATION COACH

KEN D. FOSTER

Throughout this book the key question has been: Do we evolve into the next level of human existence, or do we devolve back into the dark ages? As you have learned, we have many reasons to be hopeful. Many are waking up to the fact that they have a spark of the divine within them and realize that they can change humanity's destiny by upshifting their individual consciousness. As Ervin Laszlo says, we are not to predict a bright future. We are to create it. With this quest in mind, we are going to explore the personal transformation that will instill the seeds of positive change within you.

We are ascending to a higher age. But although the higher age will eventually come about, the level of enlightenment, the level of harmony and peace will be determined by us. The amount of conflict, destruction, war, poverty, and environmental degradation will also depend on us. We have the power to change the outcome of our current world crisis if we change our consciousness. So how do we change ourselves and attain higher consciousness now?

The answer is to awaken a longing for Self-Knowledge, which ultimately will transform the individual, family, community, nation, and the human world. As Gandhi said, "If you want to change the world, start with yourself."

But why should we change ourselves? What is the purpose of getting outside of our comfort zones and elevating our thinking to new levels of awareness? It is because we all want to realize what the Yogis refer to as ever Existence, ever Consciousness and the ever-new Bliss that opens for us the realms of higher consciousness.

If we are to obtain lasting happiness and change the world for the better, changes must take place within our thinking, habits, and actions. Now this is not an easy thing to do. Have you ever tried changing your mind when you knew that you were right, but you were not? Of course, it can be done when we are open and receptive to someone who points out our faulty thinking, but it is difficult for most people. How about changing one of your long-standing habits? It's a struggle, it can be a battle, and it takes a change in perspective, strong will, and self-discipline.

I have worked with thousands of people over the last thirty years and found that most people want to feel more connected to themselves, want to let go of fear, worry, and stress. They want to live a more abundant, fulfilling, and happy existence. But here is what is interesting: when I first talk to them, most people want to change their partners, businesses, spouses, children, and families before it dawns on them that to change anyone, they must first change their own consciousness.

The same is true of changing our world. If you ask most, they will tell you the problems we are facing in the world, including war, poverty, environmental degradation, the education systems, the government, the military industrial complex, and so on are all because of others. The truth is we are doing it to ourselves.

Years ago, a man named Covey told me we pray from God to God. It took me a while to figure out what that meant, but when I realized that the spark of the divine is in me, you, and everything, the lights went on. I realized what I do for myself will impact others in a good way, and what I do against myself will impact others in a negative way. This truth is not only on the individual level but on the macro level.

There is an old saying, "Wherever you go, you will be there." In other words, you cannot change people, places or things, before you change yourself, and if you don't change yourself, your life will be the way it is for the rest of this incarnation. This seems self-evident, but for many, it is not.

If we want to create a world that is more beautiful for everyone, then the first step is creating a new vision. We hold ourselves in high esteem, honoring the blessings that we have in our lives. We honor the sanctity of our relationships with our friends, family, and yes, our enemies too. We embrace our highest values. We step into service and use our money, power, and wisdom to contribute to the upshifting of the consciousness of those who cross our path.

We honor our bodies by keeping them healthy and fit. We educate ourselves as to what healthy and nurturing foods empower the body. We look at our homes and business environments and educate ourselves and those around us about any toxic substances that are impacting our energy.

We look at where we can conserve and live simply to use our natural resources properly. We honor Mother Earth and do our best to use sustainable products, recycle, and not pollute. We realize the oneness and brotherhood we share with the people, animals, insects, plants, trees, rivers, and oceans.

We become citizens of the world and universe. We start thinking in terms of oneness and strive to see God in all and all in God.

This kind of thinking is not natural to most, because we are coming out of the Kali Yuga (the dark ages), the lower thinking that has influenced us for several thousand years. But we can all move consistently in the direction of reimagining our bright future.

Understanding Higher and Lower Thoughts: A Journey to Self-Discovery

In the realm of self-realization and personal development, the concepts of the higher-thought and lower-thought play a significant role in understanding the duality of human nature. By delving into the aspects of the thought, we can embark on a journey of self-discovery, growth, and enlightenment.

I would like to briefly explore the qualities of the higher self and the lower self and what thoughts and behaviors we tune into when we are vibing at either aspect of ourselves.

The Higher Self:

"I want to know how God created this world. I'm not interested in this or that phenomenon, in the spectrum of this or that element. I want to know His thoughts; the rest are just details."
—Albert Einstein

The higher self is often described as the divine or spiritual aspect of an individual. It is the part of us that is connected to universal wisdom, love, and higher consciousness. When operating from the higher self, one experiences feelings of compassion, gratitude, joy, and interconnectedness with all beings. This aspect of the self is aligned with our true essence and purpose, guiding us toward personal growth, self-realization, and spiritual evolution.

Emotions of the Higher Thought:

Courage, Neutrality, Willingness, Acceptance, Openness, Love, Compassion, Peace, Joy, and Bliss.

When we experience these emotional states, we are connected to a universal field. Our actions are guided by intuition, we are in alignment with ourselves at the highest level, the infinite, immortal soul. We are following our passions, pursuing meaningful goals, in service and contributing positively to society.

The Lower Self:

Conversely, the lower self represents the egoic, materialistic, and fear-based aspects of our psyche. It is driven by desires, fears, judgments toward self and others, attachments, resistance to change, and limiting beliefs that keep us stuck in patterns of negativity, self-doubt, and separation from our true essence. When operating from the lower self, you will experience emotions such as anger, jealousy, greed, resentment, depression, and anxiety leading to a sense of disconnection from the sunlight of the spirit and others around you.

Aligning with the Higher Self Consistently

To align with our higher self, it is essential to cultivate self-awareness, mindfulness, and a sense of inner harmony. By acknowledging and transforming our lower self-tendencies, we can elevate our consciousness and embody the qualities of our higher self more fully. Practices such as meditation, yoga, journaling, and seeking guidance from coaches, spiritual teachers, or mentors can help us on this transformative journey of self-discovery.

By recognizing and embracing both aspects of ourselves, we can navigate life's challenges with greater wisdom, resilience, and compassion. As we strive to align with our higher self, we embark on a path of self-realization and spiritual growth that leads to a more fulfilling and purposeful existence.

The Nature of Thought: Individual or Universal

Have you ever wondered if the thoughts you think are coming from you or coming from somewhere outside of your brain? If we are to tune into higher realms of consciousness consistently, then we need to understand where our thoughts come from.

Are our thoughts truly our own, originating from within us as individuals, or are they part of a universal consciousness that we tap into? The debate over whether thought is individual or universal has been a topic of fascination and contemplation for philosophers, scientists, and spiritual seekers for centuries, but today we have science and insight around this topic.

Individual thought refers to the idea that our thoughts are unique to each of us as individuals, stemming from our personal experiences, beliefs, values, and memories. According to this perspective, our thoughts are generated by the complex workings of our brains and minds, shaped by our interactions with the world around us. From this viewpoint, every person is a distinct and separate entity, with their own inner world of thoughts and consciousness.

Exploring the Scientific Foundations of the Oneness of Consciousness

The concept of oneness, often associated with spiritual and philosophical traditions, posits the interconnectedness and unity of all existence. While this idea has long been a cornerstone of spiritual teachings and mystical experiences, modern science is also shedding light on the interconnected nature of the universe and the profound implications of oneness on our understanding of reality.

One of the key pillars of scientific support for the theory of oneness comes from the field of quantum physics. Quantum mechanics has revolutionized our understanding of the fundamental building blocks of reality, revealing a world that is interconnected, entangled, and nonlocal. The phenomenon of quantum entanglement, where particles become instantaneously connected regardless of distance, suggests a deep interconnectedness that transcends our conventional notions of space and time.

Building upon the insights of quantum physics, scientists have been exploring the concept of a unified field theory that seeks to explain the interconnected nature of the cosmos. This theory posits that there exists a fundamental field of energy and information that permeates all of creation, giving rise to the diverse phenomena we observe in the universe. By recognizing the underlying unity and interconnectedness of all particles, forces, and dimensions, scientists are moving toward a more holistic understanding of reality that aligns with the principle of oneness.

Neuroscience research has uncovered intriguing findings that support the idea of a collective consciousness or shared mental space. Studies on mirror neurons, empathy, and social cognition suggest that our brains are wired to resonate with the thoughts, emotions, and experiences of others, creating a web of interconnected minds that shape our social interactions and sense of empathy. This neural interconnectedness points to a deeper level of shared consciousness that transcends individuality.

The conclusion of the Vedas, written thousands of years ago, is that thought is universal, not individual. Science is now verifying this in the modern age.

The understanding that thought is universal has profound implications for how we understand ourselves and our place in the world. It suggests that we are all interconnected and that our actions and intentions have ripple effects beyond ourselves.

It also suggests that someone in Japan who is having an addiction problem may have very similar thoughts to someone in the United States of America having the same issues, since they would be tapping into the universal mind where addiction thoughts are found. Or someone who is exploring how to create a space station is tapping into the same database that other scientists who are working on the same project.

To take this further, asking the right questions in the right vibrational energy may hold the key to unlocking the power of the Universal Mind, Collective Unconscious, or Akashic records as it is called.

"If you want to know the secrets of the universe, think in terms of energy, frequency and vibration."
—Nikola Tesla

My first best-selling book was *Ask and You Will Succeed: 1001 Extraordinary Questions to Create Life-Changing Results.* From my research, when we are in the right vibrational frequency and ask powerful questions, we can access the Akashic records and get answers that are many times profound.

I have realized that stillness is the key to calming the mind. The breath and mind are interconnected. The calmer the mind, the slower the breath. I have found that when a *why* question is asked, it points us into deep purposeful answers. When a *what* question is asked, we receive creative answers. When a *when* question is asked, we tune into time-limited answers. When how questions are asked many times, the answers are slow to come unless you have experience with what you are asking for, but if you keep asking, eventually you will always get an answer.

The Sacred Quest: A Journey

Billions are living with false realities. They are living in materialistic fantasies, dependent on others to solve the issues of our time. They are unaware of how to overcome the impending challenges in their own lives and the emergencies that face our people and planet. But now, time is of the essence for them to awaken from the mass hypnosis and realize how to tap into the universal mind, remember who they are, and why they are here.

If we are waiting for our leaders to change the world, then we are waiting for the wrong person. The world will change when we collectively change. The interconnected consciousness is calling all of us to do the work to tune in and shed the old Kali Yuga consciousness.

By embracing the journey, we open ourselves to a deeper understanding of who we are at the highest level and our place in the grand tapestry of existence.

The question arises, how do we start embracing the sacred journey? Well, everyone reading this book has already started. The next step is introspection, which is the act of looking within ourselves to examine our beliefs, behaviors, and motivations. This is where intellectual understanding stops, because this is the area that takes personal motivation and courage to attain true transformation.

Introspection is the key to awakening the inner genius that resides in you. I suggest looking at the results you are getting in your life. I encourage you to rate yourself in the following areas on a scale of one to ten, with one being dismal and ten outstanding: Financial Wealth, Health, Well-being, Toxic-Free Environment, Energy, Family, Friendships, Relationships, Social Life, Spiritual, Fulfillment, Fun, Contribution, and Business.

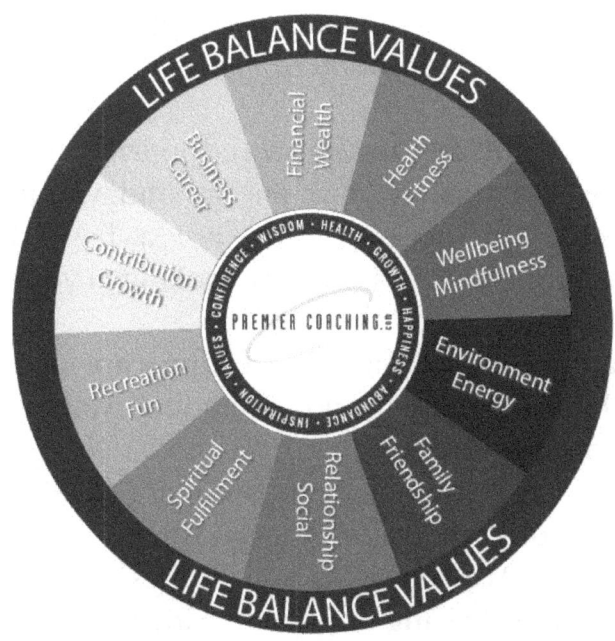

Once you have done this, focus on the first area that you are committed to changing to have a more enlightened life, and ask the following questions.

> The Eight Primary Questions for Upshifting Your Consciousness
> What are you tolerating?—Awareness
> What do you really want?—Vision
> Why will you get this no matter what?—Purpose
> What are you willing to give or give up to accomplish it?—Release
> What are the three most important steps to obtain it?—Strategies
> What could stop you from completing the vision?—Challenges
> How will you know when you are successful?—Measurement
> Who will you become as a result of getting what you want?—Evolution

Awareness is the key to the sacred journey. Expanding awareness will upshift your energy and vibration and accelerate your success. Below are a few additional thoughts in the key areas you are looking at your results.

> Health: How well are you taking care of your physical, mental, and emotional well-being? How is your diet?
> Fitness: Are you consistently doing aerobic and anaerobic exercises? Are you fit?
> Business: Are you living your values and in the business thriving or just surviving?

Career: Do you love what you do? Are you excited for your future?

Finances: Are you managing your finances wisely and with integrity, ensuring financial stability and security for yourself and your loved ones?

Relationships: Do your relationships empower you? Are you fostering connections based on mutual respect, understanding, and support?

Spiritual Life: What must happen to take your spiritual life to the next level?

Energy: How is your energy level throughout the day? Are you managing your energy effectively and engaging in practices that replenish and rejuvenate you?

Friendships: Do you surround yourself with people who uplift and inspire you? Are your friendships based on authenticity, trust, and mutual evolution?

By honestly assessing these aspects of our lives, we can gain valuable insights into areas that may need improvement and take proactive steps. By doing the inner work and recognizing the interconnectedness with personal choices, you will be stepping into a more harmonious and compassionate way of living with yourself, family, community and Mother Earth.

Upshifting Consciousness: Practical Pathways to Higher Awareness

The journey of upshifting consciousness is a transformative process that not only elevates personal awareness but also contributes to the collective evolution of humanity. This quest for higher consciousness is the key for upshifting the collective consciousness of the world. All of us have a part to play if real change is to take place.

Paramahansa Yogananda, the great Yogi and a seminal figure who brought yoga to the West in 1924, emphasized the power of meditation in upshifting consciousness. Through regular meditation practice, individuals can quiet the mind, connect with their inner self, and experience profound states of peace and clarity. Yogananda's teachings encourage the use of many techniques including Kriya Yoga to accelerate spiritual growth and enhance one's awareness. If you are not familiar with Kriya Yoga, you can find more information at Yogananda.org.

Practical Tip: Begin with daily meditation practice, even if it's just for ten to fifteen minutes. Give your body a command to relax, focus on your breath, and gently let go of any thoughts or concerns. Over time, increase the duration and explore different meditation techniques that resonate with you.

Fostering a Holistic Worldview

Ervin Laszlo advocates for a holistic worldview to elevate consciousness. He argues that recognizing the interconnectedness of all things can lead to a higher state of awareness. This perspective encourages individuals to see beyond the materialistic and fragmented view of the world, embracing instead the unity and coherence of all existence.

Practical Tip: Cultivate an awareness of interconnectedness in daily life. Practice gratitude for the natural world, recognize the impact of your actions on others, and seek to understand different perspectives. Engage in activities that promote a sense of unity, such as community service or environmental conservation.

Cultivating Intuitive Insight and Creativity

Albert Einstein delved into the realms of intuition and creativity. Einstein believed that true knowledge comes from within and that imagination is more important than knowledge. He often spoke about the role of intuition in scientific discovery, highlighting the importance of tapping into our inner creative potential to reach higher states of consciousness.

Practical Tip: Most people's intuition is undeveloped. To develop intuition, engage in activities that stimulate your creativity and intuition, such as journaling, art, or free-form brainstorming. Do things you have never done before, and allow yourself the freedom to explore new ideas without judgment. Spend time in nature, which can also enhance intuitive insights and creative thinking.

Practicing Self-Reliance and Authenticity

Ralph Waldo Emerson emphasized the importance of self-reliance and authenticity. Emerson believed that each person possesses an inner light that can guide them to truth and higher consciousness. By trusting oneself and living authentically, individuals can transcend societal limitations and connect with a deeper sense of purpose.

Practical Tip: Reflect on your highest values and purpose, then strive to align them with your actions. Practice authenticity in your interactions, speaking truthfully and acting from your true self. Let go of trying to look good or being fake and avoid conforming to societal expectations that do not resonate with your inner beliefs.

Embracing Love and Compassion

Kahlil Gibran eloquently expressed the transformative power of love and compassion in his works. Gibran believed that love is a fundamental force that elevates consciousness and connects individuals to the divine. By cultivating a heart-centered approach to life, individuals can transcend ego-driven behaviors and experience higher states of awareness and connection.

Practical Tip: Commit to acts of kindness and compassion daily. Focus on developing empathy and understanding in your relationships. Engage in loving-kindness meditation, where you silently send thoughts of love and well-being to yourself and others.

Balancing the Material and Spiritual Worlds

Swami Sri Yukteswar, Yogananda's guru, taught that achieving a balance between the material and spiritual aspects of life is crucial for upshifting consciousness. He believed that spiritual growth does not require renunciation of the material world but rather a harmonious integration of both realms. By finding this balance, individuals can lead fulfilling and enlightened lives.

Practical Tip: Evaluate your lifestyle to ensure a balance between work, leisure, and spiritual practices. Set aside time each day for activities that nourish your soul, such as meditation, prayer, or reading inspirational messages. Cultivate a sense of contentment and gratitude for what you have. Think about when enough is enough.

Harnessing the Power of Positive Thinking

Wallace Wattle's philosophy highlights the power of positive thinking and its impact on consciousness. He believed that thoughts shape reality and that maintaining a positive mindset can lead to greater clarity and higher states of awareness. This concept is also echoed in Yogananda's teachings on the power of affirmation and positive thinking.

Practical Tip: Practice positive affirmations daily. Focus on what you want to achieve and maintain an optimistic outlook. Surround yourself with positive influences and consciously shift negative thoughts to more empowering ones.

Moving Forward

"The message is simple: If you want a harmonious life and world peace, Reform Yourself."
—Ken D. Foster

If the brakes are failing in a new car, you take it back to the dealership, who not only repairs them, but notifies the factory so they can identify the problem and make sure it doesn't happen again.

So, if you want to realize world peace and harmony, then we must look at the problem. If you want a country to change, you must look at how a nation state treats other nation states. If you want to change this, then you must change the consciousness of the politicians, and for that to happen you need to change the consciousness of the people who voted for the politicians. To do this, you must change the consciousness of the individual, then when enough individuals upshift their consciousness, the global change is made automatically. The key to world peace is upshifting the individual.

In conclusion, upshifting consciousness is a multifaceted journey that involves a commitment to personal transformation, inner exploration, and a deep understanding of the interconnectedness of all life. By integrating meditation, fostering a holistic worldview, cultivating creativity, practicing self-responsibility, embodying love and compassion, seeking continuous learning, balancing the material and spiritual time, and harnessing the power of positive thinking, we can change our consciousness, restore our oneness, and become a sacred member of the great upshift movement through these practical approaches.

"In the end only kindness matters."
—Jewell

I know if each of us does the practical work described here and strives to make peace within ourselves and our family, friends, community, nation, environment, politicians, government, enemies, and all living and inanimate things on Mother Earth, the world's consciousness will upshift and change for the better.

Uniting Humanity: Wisdom and Technology for a New Era

Jon Ramer

Navigating the New Frontier: From Uncertainty to Unity

We are on an evolutionary path, moving from a "world no longer" to a "world not yet." Our goal is a wise transition, navigating our future with foresight and wisdom. The military term VUCA—Volatility, Uncertainty, Complexity, and Ambiguity—captures the essence of the challenges we face in our interconnected, rapidly changing world. It highlights the need for adaptable strategies, resilient systems, and flexible mindsets to thrive amid these turbulent conditions. This transition demands a collective response, fostering fortitude, cooperation, and innovative solutions to address our profound challenges. Our sacred covenant is clear. The pressing question is *how?*

Harmonizing with Nature: Practicing Patience and Persistence in Our Collective Dance

Ervin Laszlo writes: "We are not treating Mother Earth as our essential partner in a sacred dance. Thinking that we can dance above and beyond the bounds and possibilities of the planet is a grievous mistake. We are paying for it."

Let's build upon this metaphor. Imagine humanity as dancers, learning a new choreography. This dance symbolizes our journey to unite and restore Mother Earth. Like any new dance, it requires practice, patience, and commitment. We must embrace a new way of moving together, guided by the rhythms of nature and the wisdom it offers.

Experiment with New Patterns

Just as dancers experiment with movements to create new choreography, society must experiment with new social patterns to find more effective ways of living and working together. In order to do this, we realize we need to be synergizing humanity for regenerative unity. That means trying new ways of interacting to organize in ways that turn what we have into what we need to get what we want: a united humanity and a restored dance with Mother Earth.

Practice Together

Just as dancers practice to perfect their movements, we must commit to regular, collective efforts. This means participating in initiatives, sharing knowledge, building trust, and supporting one another in our journey.

Embrace Patience and Persistence

Learning a new dance is challenging. It takes time to synchronize our steps and move in unison. We are called to be patient with ourselves and each other, understanding that progress is made through consistent effort.

Relearn How We Learn

We must revisit and reframe our approach to learning. Nature shows us that learning is continuous and adaptive. By observing and mimicking natural processes, we can develop sustainable practices that foster unity and restoration. Nature teaches us in subtle ways. Observe how ecosystems thrive in harmony, each element playing its part in the grand performance. This is the dance we must learn—one of balance, cooperation, and mutual respect.

Harnessing Indigenous Wisdom and Ethical AI for Collective Action

In this article, we introduce a new collective practice within our One World community. Guided by the profound wisdom of Indigenous leaders and elders, particularly Patricia Anne Davis, founder of the Indigenous Wisdom Institute, we have embraced the Indigenous Ceremonial Change Process (ICCP). This process promotes constructive and life-affirming choices by reframing decision-making into an Indigenous Affirmative thinking system. The ICCP fosters win-win, constructive, and healthy outcomes, enabling group consensus and co-creative solutions, making our co-creation circles a new kind of collective practice that harmonizes modern and traditional wisdom.

At the same time, the introduction of AI has significantly altered our communication practices and expanded our possibilities for collective action. In our article, "AI Doesn't Care. We Do," we discuss the opportunities and risks of AI in our lives.

As we prepared for the symposium "Awakening to Humanity's Sacred Quest," in February 2024, we asked ChatGPT: "What would be the signs and indicators of an awakened humanity?"

ChatGPT provided 14 clear and compelling indicators, which our One World community unanimously embraced as "common sense." This experience led us to explore how the ethical use of AI can guide us in achieving group consensus and overcoming challenges to collaboration. Our goal is to set a new standard for integrating advanced technology and traditional knowledge to create ethical, impactful solutions for today's challenges.

Co-Creation Circles for Pooling and Deploying Resources

As we prepared for World Unity Week in June and the 99 Days of Peace through Unity that leads to Peace Week in September 2024, we initiated an experiment to collectively learn and grow. We formed a Community of Practice focused on learning and integrating the Indigenous Ceremonial Change Process (ICCP) with ethically used AI.

This practice aims to distill our collective insights into "wisdom pools" and facilitate group consensus, aligning our actions with the natural order of change. By combining indigenous wisdom with ethical AI, we intend to enhance our ability to think and act as one, fostering a united approach to our shared challenges and quest.

Seven Circles of Awakening: Themes for a Unified Future

We chose to organize seven Co-Creation Circles based upon the fourteen indicators of an awakened humanity. We came up with these seven themed circles:

1. Beyond Borders: Unity in Diversity and Compassion
2. Building Bridges: Global Collaboration for Peace and Equity
3. Ethics in Innovation: Technology for Human Flourishing
4. Inclusive Futures: Empowering Diversity and Social Justice
5. Sustaining Our Planet: Practices for Resilience
6. Education Revolution: Unlocking Potential for All
7. Unified Evolution: Harmonizing Collective Wisdom

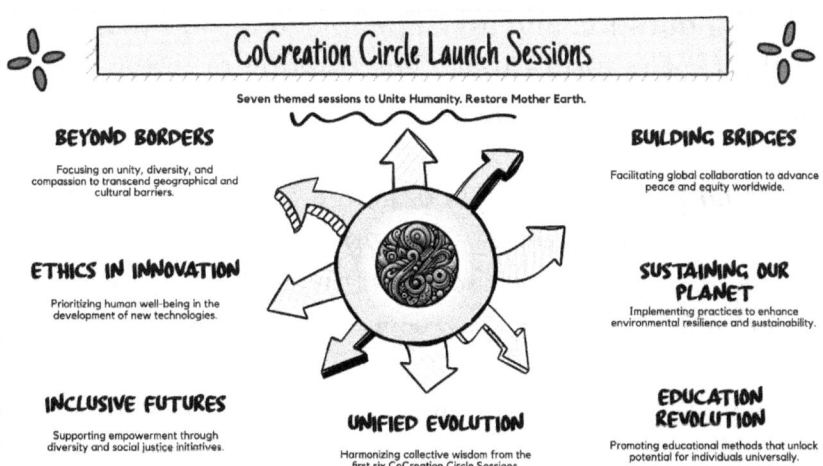

Co-Creation Circles: Crafting Solutions for a Unified Future

For each of the seven circles, we summarized an "ideal state" in other words, what would the world look like if we lived "Beyond Borders with unity in diversity and compassion?" Here's a summary of the ideal state:

> *In a united world of diversity and compassion, personal and spiritual growth promote global mindfulness, emotional intelligence, and interconnectedness. Art and creative expression celebrate diverse cultures, fostering a deep sense of global community and empathy. Solidarity movements and activism for social justice, environmental sustainability, and human rights thrive, creating a just and equitable world. We transcend borders, embrace shared humanity, and work collaboratively for the common good.*

In addition to a summarized ideal state, we formulated a framing question and asked people to answer in advance of the Co-Creation Circle. The framing question for the Beyond Borders session is:

> *What pressing global challenge are you most passionate about addressing, and how do you envision contributing to its resolution through collaborative efforts?*

Here's a summary of the over eighty answers we received:

> *The pressing global challenges people are most passionate about addressing can be unified into a cohesive vision focused on creating a just,*

sustainable, and interconnected world. Key themes include unity and collaboration, environmental regeneration, social justice, human rights, personal and spiritual growth, technological innovation for good, and creative expression and education. By integrating these themes, we aim to leverage collective intelligence and ethical action to foster a movement that promotes sustainable practices, justice, and empathy, ultimately creating a thriving and regenerative world for future generations.

We presented the summarized answers as part of the session. We used real-time feedback to gauge our level of consensus. The goal of each circle is to advance the movement from the current state to the ideal state, identifying obstacles and co-creating actionable solutions.

Harmonizing Tradition and Technology: The ICCP and Co-Creation Circles

Naming the out of balance condition and identifying the root cause is the first step in the ICCP. The ICCP emphasizes a holistic, interconnected approach, rooted in the natural elements of earth, water, fire, and air. These ceremonies foster genuine connection with the natural world and emphasize an indigenous affirmative thinking system, as described by Patricia Anne Davis. This sequence shifts individuals from a Eurocentric dualistic mindset to one that restores original, purposeful thinking and aligns with intrinsic natural connections.

Our experience with AI enriches our problem-solving and community engagement approaches. This wisdom, deeply rooted in centuries-old traditions and a profound connection to nature has shown that integrating indigenous knowledge complements and enhances our technological advancements.

In an era where collaboration and collective decision-making are paramount, #AIGroupConsensus offers an ethical and creative approach to facilitating group consensus using AI. This approach summarizes qualitative data—such as answers, suggestions, and insights—streamlining the consensus-building process and creating pools of collective wisdom. Leveraging AI makes this process more efficient, equitable, and effective.

A Movement of Movements: Co-Creating a Global Call to Action

We are refining and revising this new practice—the new dance step—we are calling Co-Creation Circles. During the 99 Days we're adding an eighth circle to focus on a demonstration project that we're calling Unite 4 Peace: A Global Broadcast and Call to Action. We will use these initial Co-Creation Circles to help us organize and coordinate an unprecedented level of collaboration and cooperation amongst those individuals, groups and organizations committed to uniting for peace.

Our quest is not a solo endeavor but a collective one—a movement of movements. Each of us brings unique steps to this dance, contributing to a diverse and vibrant choreography. We invite you to get involved and become a part of the process of cocreating our Co-Creation Circles and learning how we unite humanity to restore Mother Earth. Join us here: OneWorld.Earth.

The Principal and Contributing Authors' Bios

Ervin László is a Hungarian philosopher of science, systems theorist, integral theorist (and originally a concert pianist) who has published about seventy-five books and over four hundred papers. An advocate of the theory of quantum consciousness, Laszlo has a PhD from the Sorbonne and is the recipient of four honorary PhDs (from the United States, Canada, Finland, and Hungary). His many awards and distinctions include the Peace Prize of Japan, the Goi Award (Tokyo 2002), the International Mandir of Peace Prize (Assisi 2005), and nomination for the Nobel Peace Prize (2004 and 2005).
TheLaszloInstitute.com
ClubofBudapest.com
ErvinLaszloBooks.com

Neale Donald Walsch has written thirty-nine books on contemporary spirituality and its practical application in everyday life. Seven of the nine books in his *Conversations with God* series have made the *New York Times* Best Sellers list, with Book One remaining on that list for 134 weeks. His titles have been translated into thirty-seven languages. He is the creator of CWG Connect (www.CWGConnect.com), a global online platform connecting people who wish to more deeply explore the messages in the CWG

body of work. His latest book is *The God Solution*, published in December 2020.
NealeDonaldWalsch.com

Charles Eisenstein is an American public speaker, teacher and author. His work covers a wide range of topics, including the history of human civilization, economics, spirituality, and the ecology movement. Key themes explored include anti-consumerism, interdependence, and how myth and narrative influence culture. According to Charles, global culture is immersed in a destructive "story of separation," and one of the main goals of his work is to present an alternative "story of interbeing." He is the author of numerous essays and books, including the *Sacred Economics, Climate: A New Story,* and *The More Beautiful World our Hearts Know Is Possible.*
CharlesEisenstein.org

Jude Currivan is a cosmologist, planetary healer, futurist, and author. She is a lifelong researcher into the nature of reality, has a master's degree in physics from Oxford University specializing in quantum physics and cosmology and a PhD in Archaeology from the University of Reading in the UK researching ancient cosmologies. She has extensive experience and knowledge of world events, international politics, global economic and financial systems, and future trends. Also keeping up with the latest scientific discoveries across many fields of research, she integrates leading edge science, research into consciousness and universal wisdom teachings into a wholistic wholeworld-view.
Wholeworld-View.org
JudeCurrivan.com

Robert Atkinson, PhD, author, speaker, and developmental psychologist, is a 2017 Nautilus Book Award winner for *The Story of Our Time: From Duality to Interconnectedness to Oneness*, and a co-editor of *Our Moment of Choice: Evolutionary Visions and Hope for the Future* (2020). He is also the founder of One Planet Peace Forum, and StoryCommons, an internationally recognized authority on life story interviewing, a pioneer in the techniques of personal myth making and soul making, and a member of the Evolutionary Leaders Circle, a project of the Source of Synergy Foundation.
RobertAtkinson.net/about

Ignazio Masulli was born in Potenza in 1942. He graduated in Literature from the University of Bologna. He was a full professor of Labor History in the Faculty of Letters and Philosophy of the University of Bologna until his retirement in 2012. His scientific collaboration with the General Evolution Research Group began in 1987.

In 1993 he began collaboration with the International Club of Budapest and was cofounder of its Italian section. He is consulting editor of the magazine *World Futures* (Taylor & Francis Group, Philadelphia, PA, USA).
IgnazioMasulli.It

Alberto Villoldo is a medical anthropologist and bestselling author who has studied the shamanic healing practices of the Amazon and Andes for over thirty years. He is the founder of the Four Winds Society where he teaches Shamanic Energy Medicine. His recent books include *The Heart of the Shaman: Stories and Practices of the Luminous Warrior* and *The Wisdom Wheel: A Mythic Journey through the Four Directions*, and *Grow a New Body Cookbook*.

TheFourWinds.com

David Lorimer is a writer, lecturer, poet, and editor who is a founder of Character Education Scotland, Programme Director of the Scientific and Medical Network and Chair of the Galileo Comquest, which seeks the widen science beyond a materialistic world view. He has also been editor of *Paradigm Explorer* since 1986 and completed his one hudredth issue in 2019. Originally a merchant banker then a teacher of philosophy and modern languages at Winchester College, he is the author and editor of over a dozen books, including *Survival? Death as Transition* (1984, 2017), *Resonant Mind* (originally *Whole in One*) (1990, 2017), *The Spirit of Science* (1998), *Thinking Beyond the Brain* (2001), *The Protein Crunch*, and *A New Renaissance*.

SciMedNet.org
GalileoComquest.org

Adam C. Hall is an author, speaker, futurist, social architect, impact investor, adviser, and conservationist—with three decades as a CEO and serial entrepreneur. Adam began his professional career as a self-described Earth Conqueror, ultimately turning to the role of EarthKeeper. Committed to helping others get in touch with their innate power for personal, professional, and planetary transformation. He is the founder/CEO of the Genius Studio, creator of the Genius Process, and works particularly with accomplished leaders who are seeking more contentment, alignment, and personal meaning in their lives.

AdamHall.Solutions/about

Mirela Sula is the CEO and Founder of *Global Woman Magazine* and Global Woman Club. Mirela has worked in media and education for the last twenty years and has speaking experience from all around the world. Her background is in psychology and counseling, journalism, teaching, coaching, women's rights, and media training. Mirela is also the organizer of the Global Woman Summit and Global Woman Awards. Her last self-help book *Don't Let Your Mind Go* was a best seller and was also published in America and Turkey. Her quest is to grow her global movement and improve the future for millions of women around the world.

MirelaSula.com

GlobalWomanClub.com

Mária Sági holds a PhD in psychology from the Eötvös Loránd University of Budapest. The creator of the "Sági method" of informational healing and diagnosis, she is the author of twelve books and more than 150 articles and research papers published in Hungarian and translated into English, French, German, Italian, and Japanese. The science director for the Club of Budapest, she lives in Budapest, Hungary.

MariaSagiDr.com

Bradley Nelson (DC, ret.) is a veteran holistic physician and one of the world's foremost experts on natural methods of achieving wellness. He is the creator of the Emotion Code, the Body Code, and the Belief Code, and he is the CEO of Discover Healing, a holistic education platform that provides training and certifies practitioners worldwide.

His bestselling book *The Emotion Code* provides step-by-step instructions for working with the body's energy healing power. There are people now on every continent and in nearly every country who are using the Emotion Code to get rid of their own emotional baggage, and the best part is that they are helping their loved ones to do the same.

DiscoverHealing.com
EmotionCodeGift.com

Suzanne Giesemann is a spiritual teacher, author, and Messenger of Hope who guides people to the certainty that love never dies and that we are part of a multidimensional universe. Suzanne is a former US Navy Commander, commanding officer, and aide to the Chairman of the Joint Chiefs of Staff. Her transition from senior military officer to her current work is featured in the award-winning documentary *Messages of Hope*, based on her memoir by the same name. She has authored thirteen books and written and narrated six Hemi-Sync recordings. She produces the *Daily Way* inspirational messages read by tens of thousands each day and hosts the top-ranking weekly *Messages of Hope* podcast. She is a sought-after keynote speaker at major international conferences. Her Awakened Way app gives instant access to the *Daily Way* messages.

SuzanneGiesemann.com

Kurt Johnson has worked in professional science and comparative religion for more than forty years. A prominent figure on international committees, particularly at the United Nations. Kurt has published over two hundred scientific articles and seven books including *The Coming Interspiritual Age* and two award-winning books in science. Kurt served on the faculty of New York's Interfaith Seminary for fifteen years and was on the staff of the American Museum of Natural History in New York City for twenty-five years. As part of UNITY EARTH and the Interspiritual Dialogue Network, he co-edits two magazines: *The Convergence* and *Light on Light*, and cohosts the Convergence series on *VoiceAmerica*.
EvolutionaryLeaders.net/leaders/KJohnson

Shannon Marie Winters is an ordained interfaith-interspiritual minister, cofounder of the Light on Light Publications, and instrumental in the founding of Light on Light Press. As a scientific communications executive, Shannon also serves as managing editor, Light on Light Publications, including *The Convergence*, *Conscious Business*, and *Light on Light* e-magazines, and with the International Day of Yoga Committee at the United Nations. She is author of Joy Alchemy®, and *The Gospel of Joy*, and co-editor of, "Universal Principles and Action Steps: A historic collection gathered from organizations, networks, NGO's and thought leaders around the world."
Issuu.com/LightonLight
Lightonlight.us

Ken D. Foster is a keynote speaker, best-selling author, business strategist, and news personality, who owns a

broadcast and media production company. He is the executive producer and host of the *Voices of Courage Show* syndicated on television, podcast, plus radio broadcast in 185 countries. He specializes in working with people who are committed to leveling up their lives, maximizing their highest potential, and contributing to making the world a better place. Ken is a changemaker who pushes the envelope and challenges audiences to think differently, to see the unseeable, know the unknowable, and do the impossible.
KenDFoster.com
VoicesofCourage.us

Jon Eliot Ramer is an entrepreneur, civic leader, inventor, and musician. He is a cofounder of several collaborative technology companies including ELF Technologies, Inc., whose main solution, Serengeti, connects over seven thousand law firms with their clients and was purchased by Thomson Reuters. In 2018, Ramer formed the SINE Alliance and Network. SINE (Synergized Impact Network Exchange) is a global collaboration that fuels collective empowerment. The SINE syndicated network and social change engine amplify the positive impact of the alliance member's initiatives. SINE demonstrates how comanagement and collective capacity building can uplevel and amplify social change initiatives and their outputs, outcomes, and impacts.

Alexander Laszlo is President of the Board of Directors of the Bertalanffy Center for the Study of Systems Science (BCSSS), Director of Research at the Laszlo Institute of New Paradigm Research (LINPR), and Doctoral

Faculty in Sustainability Leadership at Fielding Graduate University. He served as the fifty-seventh President and Chair of the Board of Trustees of the International Society for the Systems Sciences (ISSS), and was Director of the Doctoral Program in Management at the Graduate School of Business Administration & Leadership (EGADE-ITESM), Mexico, and Founding Director of the Doctoral Program in Leadership and Systemic Innovation at ITBA, Argentina, where he currently resides.

As Professor of Systems Science & Curated Emergence, he teaches internationally on evolutionary leadership, collaboration, and systems thinking. He is on the editorial boards of seven internationally arbitered research journals, recipient of the Gertrude Albert Heller Award, the Sir Geoffrey Vickers Memorial Award, and the Lifetime Achievement Award for Visionary Leadership, author of over 120 journal, book, and encyclopedia publications, and a 7th Degree Black Belt in traditional Taekwon-do.

THE SACRED QUEST

BECOMING ONE ON PLANET EARTH

THE BEGINNING

www.ingramcontent.com/pod-product-compliance
Lightning Source LLC
Chambersburg PA
CBHW071701090426
42738CB00009B/1624